Through whose eyes?
Exploring racism: reader, text and context

Through whose eyes?
Exploring racism: reader, text and context

Beverley Naidoo

Trentham Books

First published in 1992 by Trentham Books Limited

Trentham Books Limited
Westview House
734 London Road
Oakhill
Stoke-on-Trent
Staffordshire
England ST4 5NP

British Library Cataloguing Publication Data
Naidoo, Beverley
 Through Whose Eyes?: Exploring Racism —
 Reader, Text and Context
 I. Title
 370.19

ISBN: 0 948080 67 1

1682998

Cover illustration by
Petra Röhr-Rouendaal

Designed and printed by Trentham Print Design, Chester and
printed in Great Britain by BPCC Wheatons Limited, Exeter.

Contents

Acknowledgements

The doctoral research on which this book is based could not have been undertaken without the help of many people. To retain their anonymity, I have created pseudonyms for the school, staff and students. While I am thus not able to acknowledge publicly people who were central to the project, my thanks are very real. I am indebted to the original Head of English at 'St Mary's' for his enthusiasm in introducing the project to the school, as well as to the Head and 'Gerald Carey', Senior Teacher, for their support during my year in the school. A special acknowledgement is due to 'Alan Parsons', who volunteered to be the project teacher, especially as the year was not an easy one for him. I am grateful to other members of staff who assisted in various ways and particularly thank the students who found themselves on the project.

Beyond the school there are numerous people and organisations to be thanked, including the two LEA Advisers (for Secondary Schools and for English) who offered me considerable support; Sarum St Michael's Educational Charity, the British Council of Churches Race Relations Unit, the LEA and the regional Arts Association for financial support; and the following for their help and participation in many different ways: David Lake and Watford Afro-Caribbean Association, Debbie Epstein, Mike Vance, John Siraj-Blatchford, Dr and Mrs Engel, Richard Finch, Olusola Oyeleye, Millie Murray, James Berry, Peter Evans, Chris Gaine, Gillian Klein, Reverend Kennedy Bedford, Sadie Kenway, Saleem Gillings, Liz Gerschel, Madeleine Lake, Iram Siraj-Blatchford, Jane Spiers, Sheila Gordon, Dr Michael Benton, Kate Allison and many others whose contributions I have valued, including not least Dr Peter Figueroa who helped me steer the obstacle course of the research. Additional thanks are due to Debbie Epstein and John Siraj-Blatchford for their helpful comments as I shaped this book and to Gillian Klein as my editor with her invaluable, indomitable optimism. Finally I should like to thank my ever patient family — especially for all those solicitously offered cups of tea.

Introduction

'Has a book ever changed your whole life?' a young man of nineteen asked me recently. He had immersed himself in reading after dropping out from a locally prestigious males-only sixth form. In the course of self-study on the dole he had come across the writings of the ancient Chinese philosopher Tao-Te Ching and it had, he said, changed his total outlook.

In my own case I could not think of any one book to which I could attribute such complete transformative power. Nevertheless many books came to mind which have certainly affected me by enlarging my vision and by writers taking me into recesses of a reality they had constructed — both social and psychological — which I had previously not entered.

The point at which one encounters a book may well be crucial, as indeed the whole manner of the encounter including those who suggest it is worth reading. For instance, there are two books and a person I associate with my decision to study Education alongside English when I first arrived in this country from South Africa in the mid-1960s. I had previously refused to consider teaching as a career and recall telling my mother that I would jump off a bridge rather than become a teacher! The photographs I took on my final day at school — of dim corridors and classrooms through darkening archways and doors — subliminally said a great deal about what I was later to articulate about my schooling. I cannot bring myself to call it 'education'. I had been an obedient and diligent schoolgirl yet in many respects my education only began after leaving school — and indeed outside, rather than inside, the classrooms of my South African university. It was a period of growing state repression and as I gradually began to see for the first time some of the stark reality all around me, I became intensely angry not only at the narrowness of my schooling, but at its complicity in perpetuating apartheid through not previously challenging my blinkered vision.

Arriving in England in the spring of 1965 — with its Dickensian rows of houses, its startling banks of yellow daffodils and the ancient Thames running under Westminster Bridge — my mind was largely tuned to writings which reflected the reality I had left behind. As the poet Dennis Brutus (1973) recorded it: 'but wailings fill the chambers of my heart/ and in my head/ behind my quiet eyes/ I hear the cries and screams'. I had been offered a place at the University of York and a letter awaited me in London. It was from Harry Rée, then Professor of Education at York. It contained an introduction to an Education Officer in Hertfordshire who might be able to find me a temporary teaching post for a term. With little money to hand, I followed it up.

More significant, however, was what seemed a casually phrased question about whether I had considered including Education within my degree... and, by the way, had I come across Camara Laye's *The African Child* and Edward Blishen's *Roaring Boys?* I read them and was hooked. The contexts were both so different — Laye's memories of a West African childhood and Blishen's semi-autobiographical novel of a young teacher's initiation into the violence of schooling and youth culture in London's East End. What was in those texts that enticed me in? I cannot attempt to recall specific responses twenty-seven years on but, dipping once again into those books, I warm to each author's distinct voice. Within each of them I hear a strong, implicit commitment to education as a process of opening out and questions being raised about the nature of schooling, power, young people and society... some of the very questions, along with those about how learning takes place, which are currently derided by those in power as 'academic'.

This book tells the story of a year spent with a class of young white people, in a predominantly white area, engaged in reading literature written from perspectives strongly indicting racism. It is about their written responses as well as the discussions among themselves and with their teacher. It is also about their work with visitors, in particular black artists. As such, this is a book about educational practice. Since this gives rise to questions, reflections, hypotheses and suggestions for future practice, *Through Whose Eyes?* is inextricably involved in thinking and theorising about learning. The classroom research formed the basis for a doctoral thesis entitled *Exploring Issues of Racism with White Students through a Literature-based Course* (Naidoo 1991) and I have attempted in both the original thesis and this book to retain — at their core — voices from within the classroom.

For those teachers and librarians who have already taught or recommended some of the works used on the year's course, this book invites reflection on their own experiences of young people's encounters with such texts. I further hope that those who are not already familiar with some of the works will want to try them out as well as other texts which contain the challenges of culturally diverse literature. Perhaps it will also be of interest to other writers for young people who, like myself, are curious about both sides of the literary transaction and the question of 'through whose eyes' readers read. I particularly hope, however, that the readership of this book will extend beyond the domain of 'English' to include all those who want to enable young people and schools to play a more positive role in constructing a just society.

Chapter One

Racism, reading and the project

'those kinde of people': defining racism

'there are of late divers blackamoors brought into this realme, of which kinde of people there are already here to manie... her Majesty's pleasure therefore ys that those kinde of people should be sent forth of the lande...'

So spoke Queen Elizabeth I through her Privy Council in 1596 (Acts of the Privy Council, XXVI, 1596-7). The immigration debate is not new to Britain. The burgeoning slave trade of the 16th and 17th centuries saw the arrival of increasing numbers of black people into England, largely as servants and slaves. Desired only for their labour, they were clearly perceived by the native English as different in 'kinde' and quite distinguishable from 'people of our owne nation'.

The roots of racism lie deep within British history. Echoes of the concepts, language and agenda of Elizabeth I's Privy Council reverberate nearly 400 years later in pronouncements of politicians of the last two decades.[1]

While there is a subtle shift from the language of overt racial superiority to that of cultural difference, there still remains a widely-held 'common-sense' notion that people have biologically distinguishing features which separate one 'race' from another. This idea persists despite the evidence that 'race' itself has no objective biological validity (Hiernaux et al 1965; Rose et al 1978; Lewontin 1987). Scientists tell us that there is greater biological variation within any designated racial group than between any two such groups. 'Race' is in fact a product of the human mind and behaviour —in other words, a social construction (Figueroa 1984; 1991). Stuart Hall has given us a useful analogy in likening it to a lens through which people view and experience reality.[2]

While racism is evident in many societies and not unique to Britain, it has strong historical roots in this country, maintaining common elements — or an 'echo' — over time. However it is also historically specific to each period (Hall 1978), its 'shape' adapting to new conditions. In its structural form it is deeply embedded at an institutional level within our economic, political and social structures, policies and practices. In its ideological form it is deeply embedded within popular culture (Mullard 1980) and within what Peter Figueroa (1984) has termed the society's 'frames of reference'. Shared by the majority of Britons and closely associated with British identity, these frames of reference are the 'largely unacknowledged and unverbalised substratum of beliefs, assumptions, feelings, quasi-memories, etc. which underlie, sustain and inform perception, thought and action' (Figueroa and Swart 1986).

My understanding of racism is that it is more complex than is suggested by the 'racism = power + prejudice' formula. The latter has tended to promote a personalised and simplistic notion of power in which, for instance, it has been argued that all white people in Britain have power over black people and only white people can be racist.[3]

In other words, whiteness or biological skin colour becomes the pre-eminent critical factor for any social analysis concerning black/white relationships. Yet power is clearly also a function of features such as class, gender, sexuality and able-bodiedness, as well as 'race', and the operation of power in black/white interactions may be both complicated and dynamic or shifting when these come into play. Furthermore there is no room within the simplified 'power + prejudice' formula for Gramsci's concept of hegemony and the way power is maintained partially through the compliance of the oppressed (Gramsci 1971), nor for the way in which language shared by oppressor and oppressed plays a key role in this process.

My own working definition of racism is a broad one. It was sufficient to the purpose of my study to conceive of racism as a highly complex phenomenon of discrimination and oppression, which is historically specific in both its structural and ideological forms in each society, and which is based on, as well as sustained by, a socially-constructed belief in the existence of inherently different 'races'. Language not only plays a key role in reflecting racism within the society but in transmitting and constructing the racist frames of reference which help perpetuate it.

In Britain conceptions of 'race' are currently shaped within the duality of a highly efficient framework of nationality and immigration legislation — promoting 'British' equals 'white' —and constrained Race Relations legislation, attempting to counter some of the racist effects of the former. The same duality can be seen within education. The 1988 Education Reform Act furthers divisions between schools, particularly between those that 'have' and those that 'have not', thus reinforcing black disadvantage, inequality and injustice (Verma 1990; Richardson 1988, 1989; Hatcher 1989; Ball and Troyna 1989). Whatever useful statements we may find within the National

Curriculum reflecting Britain as a diverse society — and which contrast strongly with its fundamental nationalism elsewhere — it would be naive to disregard the over-arching discriminatory effects of the Education Reform Act.

However, it is precisely because there are contradictions that there is room for manoeuvre. Given the role of schools in the business of cultural transmission (Lawton 1973; Bowles 1976; Bourdieu 1976), it is quite unrealistic to conceive of schools having the power of directly changing structures in society. Nevertheless the curriculum is not monolithic and space still remains for teachers and students to question and challenge contradictions. Developing a school culture in which racist frames of reference are questioned is an important contribution to the roles students will be capable of taking on beyond the school gates, both in the present and the future.

Why focus on a predominantly white area?

According to the Commission for Racial Equality (1988), the perpetuators of racist abuse within schools are not a lunatic fringe but 'ordinary, everyday members of the learning community' spanning students, staff and parents. Although actual instances of overt racist abuse are reduced in predominantly white areas where there are fewer black and ethnic minority students — perhaps partly accounting for the ubiquitous 'no problem here' response from teachers in such places (Gaine 1987) — there is consistent evidence of the persisitence of wide-spread racist attitudes amongst young white people (British Social Attitudes 1984; Swann Committee 1985; Williams 1986; Tomlinson 1990). Furthermore, as Stuart Hall points out, racism is as much 'a structured absence, a not speaking about things, as it is a positive setting up of attitudes to 'race'.' (Hall 1985). A major issue for curriculum development concerned with combating racism is indeed that of marginalisation. While white institutions and power structures in inner cities and provincial towns with significant black populations have at least been challenged over the past couple of decades to concede some shifts in political power, leading among other things to certain shifts in local education policies, the situation is different in predominantly white areas. And as Bill Taylor reminds us 'the majority of Britain's population... does not live in inner cities' (Taylor 1984: 1).

My decision to devise a project with literature at its core, for a school in a predominantly white area, was undertaken in full knowledge of the limitations of addressing racism in isolation, compared with change throughout the whole of a school's formal and informal curriculum. Nevertheless, as an outside individual (without a potential school in mind at the outset), I felt I had a reasonable chance of interesting a school in undertaking a university-linked research project relating to a literature course within its English department, compared with no chance at all of persuading a school to initiate a program of complete reform. It was certainly my hope, however, that the project itself might act as a catalyst in raising wider implications for the school as a whole.

Literature and the reading process

However, apart from the question of feasibility, there is the question of 'why literature'? As I see it, literature's prime quality is the ability to carry human voices across time, place, experience, society, culture. Having been brought up as a white, middle-class South African child — with all that entailed in terms of the construction of blinkered, racist childhood perceptions — I have personally found books written by writers from very different backgrounds a major resource in enabling me to listen to other voices. Significant literature, to me, is that in which the lives of characters are represented in relation to deep currents in their society. Characters are contextualised, so that in so far as one observes them or empathises with them, one can learn something of what it is to be human in that time, that place, those circumstances. Literature is political and one's choice of literature is political, although the reader may of course ignore, or simply not see, the meanings that are there.[4]

My own belief in the potential power of literature is summed up in my introduction to an anthology explicitly concerned with young people coming into social and political consciousness (Naidoo 1987):

> Literature has the tremendous quality of allowing us to engage imaginatively in the lives of others. It enables us to move beyond ourselves and our own experiences. If we allow ourselves to respond to it fully, it can be a great educator. For those of us brought up monoculturally, literature which springs from outside our own boundaries can be a life-line.

This remains a statement largely of potential. In questioning what it is in a text that invites or inhibits a reader, Margaret Meek writes that 'it is not necessary for him (sic) to recognise his social milieu in the setting, but to find his interior fiction as part of a writer's intention' (Meek 1980: 36). One of my criteria for selecting key texts for the research project was that although some of the settings might be alien to the readers, the texts should contain enough points of connection for the readers to enable an imaginative leap and reveal a certain universality of 'interior fiction'. Both literature and drama offer a 'legitimate' arena for students to take on, at least temporarily, another 'reality'. According to Tolkien (1964), the reader enters into a 'Secondary World' created by the writer.[5]

Furthermore, in the role of 'spectator' or 'onlooker' (Harding 1962) in this Secondary World, the reader is involved in not only responding to, but evaluating, what she or he perceives. As with the writer in the process of writing, the degree of reader involvement or detachment, conscious or unconscious engagement, retrospection or anticipation within the story is individually variable (Benton 1983). Thus thirty students reading a story might be seen to produce thirty different readings. This does not preclude, however, the existence of common sources of difficulty in interpretation as investigated by James Squire (1964),[6] nor the fact that those personal readings are likely to have been framed within shared cultural contexts. Our separate personal lives, as we are reminded by Terry Eagleton, are 'determined by a wider public one' (Eagleton 1985: 7). Part of that framing also relates to the very manner in which a text is approached, for example the kind of expectations students may have of a 'literary' text (Gilbert 1987). [7]

Elizabeth Freund points out that one thing in common between different theories of reader-response is the assumption that 'the practice of supposedly impersonal and disinterested reading is never innocent and always infected by suppressed or unexamined presuppositions' (Freund 1987: 10).[8] In other words, no text is self-sufficient. Louise Rosenblatt (1938) has been asserting for over fifty years against those critics ('the formalists') who would prioritise the text, that reading is a transaction between reader and text:

> ...the term transaction, as I use it, implies that the reader brings to the text a network of past experiences in literature and in life. (The author's text also is seen as resulting from a personal and social transaction...) In the reading situation, the poem — the literary work — is evoked during the transaction between reader and text (Rosenblatt 1985: 35).

'We read what we are' or 'we are what we read'?

While individual readings or 'evocations' of the text are in one sense unique, they will, however, also reflect certain common cultural assumptions on the basis of common frames of reference developed within a society.[9] Given that racism —with apartheid one of its most extreme manifestations —segregates our experiences both physically and mentally in varying degrees, I have been particularly curious to examine the effect of racist frames of reference on the reading of fiction. As a writer of children's fiction attempting to bring alive something of both the oppression and resistance of black South African children (which I myself never perceived as a child), I see myself using my imagination as a weapon against that segregation (Naidoo 1985; 1989). Indeed I hope to take my readers into narratives and on journeys which will involve them in asking questions and challenging injustice, at least mentally, through being absorbed in the story. What actually happens as they read and what happens when they leave the story is something I do not know, although I do at times receive letters from individual readers which reveal questions spilling over into life.[10] So although by studying or deconstructing a writer's work we may perceive certain 'messages', hidden or otherwise, within it, how individual readers receive those messages can be problematic.

A comprehensive review of research for the American National Council of Teachers of English on reader-responses to literature indicates readers' preferences for works to which they feel they can relate personally (Purves and Beach 1972). Identification with a character or situation appears to lead easily to projection, with a reader imputing values and supplying background not contained in the text. Furthermore, reading material conflicting with a reader's world view is liable to be misinterpreted, with readers being highly selective in their interpretation.[11] In her important study on a wide range of research into the relationship between reading and prejudice, Sara Goodman Zimet comments:

> Both personal testimony and empirical research strongly suggest that while our attitudes, values and behaviours may be influenced by what we read, when left to our own initiative we read what we are. In other words, we select our reading to support our predispositions rather than in order to change them (Zimet 1976: 17).

The critical qualification here is, however, 'when left to our own devices' and Zimet offers evidence of studies suggesting that it is possible to modify attitudes and behaviour so that 'we are what we read'. It is the circumstances under which the reading is done (including, for example, related teaching) which she claims 'will determine which will have the greatest impact, the reader or the printed message' (ibid).

Studies of reading and 'attitude change'

As one might expect, studies of attitude change related to young people's reading have produced variable results depending on a range of circumstances (Zimet 1976; Lynch 1987). The majority of these reported studies have had positive if limited outcomes, although it is not possible to know to what extent the young people whose attitudes 'improved' were not simply showing more sensitivity to what they felt was 'expected' on re-test. It is also apparent that without reinforcement in the child's total environment, any positive attitude change is also likely to disappear rapidly (Zimet 1976; Festinger 1964). A major drawback of these studies which claim positive results is the lack of data on long-term effects.

A further issue relates to whether one can separate the effect of particular teachers from that of the particular books to which they have introduced their pupils. While Zimet points to a number of studies, based on personal testimony, which confirm how some adults and children perceive themselves to have been influenced by key books, the challenging educator Harry Rée — in a piece written shortly before his death —inextricably connected certain memorable teachers and literary influences:

> ...I recognise that my philosophy of life and even the career I chose to follow were largely determined by such reading — or should I say, by such men? (Rée 1991).

Given that a relationship with a teacher might continue over a period of time, the relationship itself might, in the right circumstances, provide a reinforcing framework to support individual reperception.

The contextualising of reading and readers

Investigations since those reported by Zimet have tended to move away from the limited traditional 'laboratory' design of test, experiment, re-test, to an ethnographic focus on the actual process of students' written and verbal responses in the classroom at the time of reading. The shift towards ethnography indicates increasing recognition of the complexity not only of the reading process as a transaction between reader and text, but of locating the question of attitudes and attitude change in a total social context. The ethnographer takes a holistic approach in investigating the situation as it is and discovering what is problematic, rather than attempting to control selected variables according to a pre-specified coding system (Delamont and Hamilton 1986; Hammersley 1983).

In a study of Robert Jeffcoate teaching Dickinson's *The Devil's Children* (1971) to a majority white, multi-ethnic first year secondary class, Kathy Stredder (1978) concludes with the necessity of examining the hidden curriculum; the teacher's role and teaching methods, particularly in providing situations in which students can explore and communicate their own feelings; and the role and involvement of researchers and teachers in collaborating on curriculum innovation.[12]

Veronica Treacher (1983; 1984/5), combining the role of teacher and researcher, provides self-critical and valuable insight into interactions and responses in a majority white, multi-ethnic class of fourth year boys with whom she read Richard Wright's powerful autobiography *Black Boy* (first published 1945). Her intention was to examine how literature might increase understanding between the different ethnic groups in the class. In particular she 'wanted an improved awareness on the part of the white boys of the historical position of the blacks' (Treacher 1983: 9). Confronted by the embarrassment and vulnerability of black students in the class, through the novel's exposure of black pain and degradation, Treacher re-examined her own position of control as a white, middle-class teacher and her traditional pedagogy of teacher-led discussions. On the one hand she had been attempting to fulfil a complete Humanities programme in one isolated English project, while on the other she had used her traditional authority to side-step any potentially confrontational current issues of racism. Furthermore the 'historical and sociological explanations often shifted the emphasis from the narrative where, observably, the book's meanings were most accessible' (1984/5: 24). Veronica Treacher recommends the need for teachers to create space for students to express their views openly and to connect with their students' experiences.[13] Black literature, according to Treacher, also needs to be introduced in the context of language of resistance.

A fascinating account by Paul Cosway and Carmen Rodney (1987) of teaching Jan Needle's *My Mate Shofiq* (1979) interweaves their dual perspectives as a white and a black teacher respectively, working together with fourth year all-white secondary students who were encouraged to be honest in both verbal and written responses. Carmen Rodney (who had strong reservations about using this book from the start because of its stereotypical portrayal of Shofiq's family) notes that the students' written responses did not reflect the racism of the discussions. In the latter, racist comments were made by a minority, who were the most vocal students, outweighing the larger but quieter number of more tolerant pupils.

Cosway and Rodney's account examines where readers are placed in the text — alongside the white protagonist who gradually discards his racist perceptions — but the teachers find no evidence of readers with strongly racist frames of reference similarly shifting. In other words, these readers did not appear to fulfil the role of what Wolfgang Iser (1978) defined as the text's 'implied reader'. Indeed Carmen Rodney believes the book reinforced opinions in the class, with the tolerant becoming slightly more tolerant and the intolerant becoming more prejudiced, dismissing any challenge as 'fiction'. It appears that those with no definite opinions at the beginning tended towards a slightly more tolerant view. In other words:

> The effect of the book, it seems, varies widely according to the sensitivity of the reader, the sophistication (necessary in order to recognise the irony) and the degree of prejudice with which the text is approached (Cosway and Rodney 1987: 23).

In addition, Paul Cosway questions the effect of a number of other common set-books written with a similar structure by white writers — where a white protagonist begins with a negative view of black people but is gradually 'sensitized', coming to recognise a common humanity.

Sandra Hann (undated) has also reported on *My Mate Shofiq* (one of the most contentious of children's fiction texts of recent years) in a useful study of reader-responses by middle and secondary students in a multi-ethnic area, as part of a 'Fiction and Multicultural Education' project. With the readers in the project self-selected and well-motivated, Hann noted differences in response to a range of texts in terms of various factors such as the children's background and cultural preconceptions, age and experience, including their experience as readers. Sandra Hann suggested age and reader-sophistication to be significant factors in how children responded to Needle's novel, with older readers being better able to perceive the author's intention in explicitly showing racism.

The research project

The form my own research project took — with a particular focus on the responses of the students as readers — developed partly out of my curiosity as a writer attempting to uncover something of 'the reader as ideologist' (Hollindale 1988). How do readers' frames of reference affect their reading and the ways in which they follow or diverge from the paths offered to them within texts as 'implied readers'? My notion of reading accords closely with Louise Rosenblatt's model of the writer and reader each contributing their own 'network of past experiences' (Rosenblatt 1985: 35) and frames of reference in the transaction. I was furthermore attracted by the possibilities of reader-response study and an ethnographic approach, as characterised by Michael Benton (1988: 27-9): reflexivity of the researcher who forms part of the phenomena as a 'participant' rather than an 'objective' observer; recognition of the context of reading; description leading to the theorising of the process of response; and flexibility of enquiry, given that one is not tied to testing out a preconceived theory.

My original aims were to investigate the potential for certain works of literature which contain strong indictments of racism from the writer's perspective to extend white students' empathies; to challenge ethnocentric and racist assumptions and concepts; and to develop critical thinking about the nature of our society. By using various reader-response strategies I hoped to uncover something of the reading transactions amongst a class of white teenage readers. Apart from the personal perceptual filters through which each student would view and respond to a text, could I detect the workings of a more common filter connected with 'race'? My concern was not only to uncover the students' frames of reference but to observe whether any apparent shifts occurred in these frames through their reading of the selected texts, through discussions, or through other specific interventions related to the texts.

I proposed, therefore, to set up a year's course of literature for an all white class of Year 9 (then third year) secondary students through which issues of racism could be explored, with the selected books all being written from a perspective strongly indicting racism. I would not be the teacher but a participant observer who collaborated with the teacher, my presence being explained to the class in terms of my interest in their responses to the literature they would be reading. The students were not, however, to be informed that I was a writer of books for young people and I did not wish them to be told explicitly about my interest in racism, although it was likely that the latter would emerge as the year progressed. I felt this partial explanation of the research would be justified on two counts. Firstly, I did not wish the students to falsify or tailor their responses (albeit unconsciously), either in terms of my perceived interest or what they might feel to be 'appropriate'. Secondly, it was important that the course be perceived in terms of mainstream literary standards and not one only relevant to an exploration of racism.

At the outset I had five main objectives. The first was to establish initially what were the significant frames of reference amongst the students in relation to 'race'. I envisaged a survey (not to be associated in the students' minds with the course) which would provide me with a limited amount of quantitative information that might not otherwise come to light and which might prove of use in interpreting some of my qualitative findings.

Secondly, using selected works of literature, I intended to develop, in collaboration with the teacher, ways of exploring these texts which encouraged empathy with the perspective of characters who were victims of racism but who resisted it. There was to be a strong emphasis on students responding directly to the texts, for example in reading journals and in small group discussions. I wanted them also to explore themes in drama related to those being raised in the literature.

Thirdly, I wanted to bring in relevant visitors, especially black artists, to work with the students, as an important element in the project. Fourthly, it was my intention to document and monitor the processes at work, particularly those which indicated any change in perceptions, or obstacles to change. Finally, I intended to gather the students' evaluations of the year's course and at the end of the project to investigate whether there was any notable change in their frames of reference relating to 'race'.

While literature remained at the core of the course, towards the end of the year, circumstances led to a new direction and issues of racism were addressed directly with the students without the intervening medium of fiction. This move from fiction to 'real life' provided a new and contrasting dimension in which to study student responses.

As an action-researcher I acknowledged a dual role. On the one hand, as activator and instigator of the project, I had devised a year's course of literature which I hoped would have the maximum chance of challenging racist frames of reference. On the other hand, as researcher, I was required to observe as accurately and fully as possible what seemed to be occurring. Both roles involved subjective judgement and this study is largely ethnographic in character. My intended primary focus was to be on the interaction of students and texts. Recognising the close web of content and context, when devising my research, I had envisaged a collaborative learning framework within the class — one in which the students would not feel 'overweighted' by the teacher's authority (Hall 1981).

In the event, although the reader-response methodology ensured a certain amount of space for students to express themselves without being directly led by the teacher, the classroom I found myself observing was far more traditionally teacher-centred than I had anticipated. I thus rapidly found my intended primary focus widening from that of students and texts to one encompassing the context of the traditional classroom in which the texts were being presented and 'constructed'. The classroom in turn could not be extrapolated from the school, nor the school from the society.

Outline of chapters

Having provided the background and rationale of my research in this chapter, in Chapter Two I aim to give a brief overview. This includes the school and classroom context; a survey of racist perceptions amongst the students, carried out before and after the project; and an outline of the course. Chapters Three to Six focus largely on the students' responses to four novels. Chapter Seven looks at some of the approaches to the texts through drama. Chapter Eight examines the students' responses as the focus shifted from fiction to reality through a television series and a week of drama workshops involving visitors concerned with racism in their working lives. In Chapter Nine I present my conclusions, raising some of the problems and possibilities in challenging racism for teachers.

I should point out that my original research thesis is considerably longer than this book. While I aimed to retain my general findings intact, it has been necessary to prune somewhat drastically. Apart from having to pare down examples of the students' interactions — for instance with the texts, their teacher, the visitors and each other — I have also omitted several discrete areas in this book, such as the detailed findings of the two Racist Perceptions Surveys and the science session on classification aimed at questioning the validity of 'race'. The thesis is available for those who wish to explore such areas in more detail (Naidoo 1991). My hope is that readers will indeed identify yet other 'gaps' and unanswered questions which they wish to fill for themselves — by engaging in their own processes of action and further research, however small-scale, into how young people can become engaged in challenging injustice and inequality. I shall be delighted if this book serves that purpose.

Notes to Chapter 1

1 'The nation has been, and is still being, eroded and hollowed out from within by implantation of unassimilated and unassimilable populations... alien wedges in the heartland of the state' (Powell, 9.4.76, in Gilroy 1987: 43).

'People are really rather afraid that this country might be rather swamped by people with a different culture and you know the British character has done so much for democracy, for law, and done so much throughout the world, that if there is any fear that it might be swamped, people are going to react and be rather hostile to those coming in' (Thatcher, 30.1.1978).

2 Describing the crisis of the 1970s economic recession, Stuart Hall wrote: 'This is not a crisis of race. But race punctuates the crisis. Race is the lens through which people come to perceive that a crisis is developing. It is the framework through which the crisis is experienced' (Hall 1978: 31).

3 'In short, the racism = power + prejudice formula rests on a personalized view of power and an understanding of racism which sets it aside from economic relations. White power and white attitudes within particular institutions become the focus of policies. The political implications of this are far reaching' (Carter and Williams 1987: 174).

4 Even animals are political! How many adults passing on 'Brer Rabbit' tales explore with children how they connect to traditional African tales (of the little rabbit surviving against mightier forces by his wits) and the meanings these tales might have held for the black slaves who re-made them in America? See Julius Lester's introduction to his retelling of *The Tales of Uncle Remus* (1987).

5 However I suspect Tolkien's conception of a Secondary World is different from that of a writer directly exploring social reality through fiction. Whereas Tolkien refers in his piece 'On fairy stories' (1964) to the reader's move back out into the Primary World in terms of 'the spell is broken: the magic, or rather art, has failed', the writer exploring social reality may actually want the reader to move back and forth between the two worlds, raising questions about both.

6 In his study *The Responses of Adolescents While Reading Four Short Stories*, Squire (1964) identified six sources of difficulty creating problems for adolescents in reading fiction: failure to grasp the meaning; reliance on stock responses; 'happiness binding' or the desire for a happy outcome; critical predispositions such as that the story should be 'true to life'; irrelevant associations; the search for certainty.

7 Gilbert views readers as 'situated in culturally determined discursive traditions, and the effects of these traditions determine the nature of the reading a text will be given and the meaning assigned to it' (1987: 245).

8 The point is vividly made by two lines she quotes from a poem by Wallace Stevens, 'Phosphor Reading by His Own Light': 'It is difficult to read. The page is dark./Yet he knows what it is that he expects.'(Freund 1987: 2)

9 Rosenblatt's early work, *Literature as Exploration* (1938), written during the rise of Naziism, shows considerable awareness of personal response being shaped within the wider society.

10 From my writer's perspective I certainly like to think that literature can be more than Eagleton's (1985) 'moral technology', whose liberal humanist function in modern capitalist society is to promote depoliticised sensitivity by producing 'an historically peculiar form of human subject who is sensitive, receptive, imaginative

and so on... about nothing in particular' (1985: 5). The writer Chinua Achebe (1989), commenting on the decision of a retired German judge not to retire to a lucrative consultancy in pre-independent Namibia after reading Achebe's novel *Things Fall Apart*, also questions 'the fashionable claim made even by writers that literature can do nothing to alter our social and political condition. Of course it can!'

11 This bears out Festinger's (1957) theory of cognitive dissonance. Festinger proposed that people will not attend to that which they perceive is dissonant with their present frame of reference, although Hatt (1976) argues that this avoidance is not as universal as Festinger suggests.

12 Dickinson's *The Devil's Children* (1970) is a futuristic novel about survival, involving a band of Sikhs and a small white English community. Robert Jeffcoate's own account can be read in *Positive Image* (Jeffcoate 1979: 92-6). The evaluation by Kathy Stredder is particularly interesting given Jeffcoate's stated concern not to interfere with the attitudes of his students. His objectives reveal the confusion in his thinking about teacher 'neutrality', namely 'that the white children should come to understand and respect another way of life' at the same time as intending 'to explore the children's reactions without necessarily wanting, in any primary sense, certain outcomes rather than others' (Stredder 1978: 84-5).

13 The need for an ethos of openness is eloquently stressed by Robin Richardson (undated) and the need to connect with students' own experiences underlined by both Chris Searle (1977) and Stuart Hall (1981).

Chapter Two

Setting the context

The school

The project was set up in a county where there is no significant black community to challenge monocultural and racist complacency and to create pressure for change. With very little activity concerning multicultural/anti-racist education in the county at the time, I was fortunate to find a voluntary-aided comprehensive Church school for 11-16 year olds, St Mary's, which was willing to take on the project. While the school had no specific policy relating to issues of equality, the senior management was in the process of reviewing and consulting staff on a statement of the school's philosophy and its ethos as a Christian establishment. This included references to 'racism or any other form of social division' as 'totally unacceptable' and to the importance of developing in pupils a sense of justice. The Headteacher identified the school's most fundamental value as being that of individual freedom.

St Mary's drew its students from a wide area, suburban and rural, and was predominantly white and relatively affluent. There were no black teachers and in a student body of over 1000 students, only about half a dozen were black. A key factor in St Mary's accepting the project was the enthusiasm of its Head of English, a man who was openly committed to challenging racism. His support was crucial in having it accepted by the school and the English department. He was keen to be the project teacher, and almost certainly would have been had he not received promotion to another school. In the preparatory period from January to July 1988, while he was still at St Mary's, he helped set up a series of formal and informal meetings with teachers within and beyond the department which created a sense of anticipation and openness to change. Given his personal commitment to developing education for equality and justice, the outcomes both within the classroom and in the wider school would very possibly have been different had he remained. The Head of St Mary's also placed great store on the ability of the Head of English to spark interest and concern in other staff, seeing the project as a practical catalyst for raising issues of equality and racism within the school as a whole. However the school's major structures were hierarchical and departmental, and with the departure of the 'insider innovator', there appeared to be no other real strategy for dissemination. From the perspective of an outsider, the staffroom communicated a sense of individual enclaves with little real cross-curricular activity in evidence. The teachers were already experiencing major change in the implementation of a faculty structure and were beginning to gird themselves for the National Curriculum. Furthermore the Head was sensitive to staff resistance towards any move seen as a 'top-down exercise', hence his reliance on the charisma of the outgoing Head of English to initiate interest in the ideas behind the project.

Despite the school's strong statement against racism, at ground-level in practice as opposed to rhetoric, it was clear that discussion about racism was seen as 'sensitive' territory. I sensed this for myself within the staffroom and, given the locality, it would have been unusual not to have found teachers who revealed a range of racist perceptions generally current within the wider society. Extreme examples were rare and I heard of them at second hand. For instance, in the term leading up to the project, a couple of teachers launched an open verbal attack on the Head of English that he was engaging in indoctrination of pupils and that if Enoch Powell had had his way, there would not be any problem now! More common were the kind of remarks revealing less conscious racist perceptions, for example, a reference by a science teacher to his previous inner-city classes as 'liquorice all-sorts' and by an English teacher to a 'multicultural book-box' as being about 'children from other countries'. The same teacher expressed reluctance to use Rosa Guy's *The Friends* (1977), because her responsibility was to teach students to write in standard English with 'proper' sentence structure.

After the departure of the Head of English, there was unfortunately no forum, not even within the English department, where such issues could actually be discussed and opened out. Pressured coffee breaks with snatched conversations did not provide that. Certainly the English department contained people who, had circumstances been different, would have been able to play a positive, collaborative role in addressing racism. From my outsider perspective, the sense of separate subject departments following their own particular courses was mirrored within the English department itself, with a sense of individuals each largely doing 'their own thing'. Thus during the project year itself, not only the work, but the ideas behind it, seemed territorially contained for the most part within the confines of one classroom.

The teacher

In devising the project it was necessary to be flexible. Ideally I should have chosen to work with a teacher with whom I shared similar ways of thinking about racism and how it operates, as well as similar ways of thinking about education. We should then have been able to collaborate on the basis of a shared frame of reference, reflecting back to each other our perceptions as the project progressed. However the chance of finding someone with whom I shared that degree of common ground was fairly limited, and from the beginning I had offered to work with anyone who was prepared to take on the project knowing my agenda. I felt that would at least create sufficient basis for collaboration.

Furthermore the methodology proposed for reader-response work was essentially collaborative and non-authoritarian, enabling students to explore and share their responses rather than being directed what to think. Given that methodology, I envisaged my major focus could remain largely trained on the students and their interactions with the texts and other inputs. It was my hope, however, that the teacher would engage in exploration alongside the students, be open to new insights, and be prepared to shift where possible from centre stage to playing a more complex role in creating the space for challenges and questions to arise amongst the students themselves.

Given actual events and the departure of the Head of English, I was relieved that another member of the English department at St Mary's volunteered to take on the project. Alan Parsons, Head of Drama, stated that he was interested in the course I proposed because it appeared 'innovative'. He was enthusiastic about the reader-response methodology, talking in a pre-project interview of the dangers of a mode of teaching in which students simply reproduce the teacher's views. Having undergone change in his own drama methodology, he felt this was now extending him into questioning whole aspects of schooling with its 'extremely formalised relationships' and structures which were 'fundamentally dehumanising'. He was also keen to see whether it was possible to measure the effects of 'a specific preoccupation', although not necessarily that of racism. He further acknowledged not to have thought much about issues of racism but said he was increasingly intolerant of it, having become much more alert to it through the influence of the out-going Head of English.

While it was clear that Alan was an extremely hard-working, committed teacher, once the classroom stage was underway it was soon apparent that he did not bear out the assumptions I had made about the likely teaching methodology of a teacher volunteering to run the course. Nor did his practice reflect the kind of critical questioning that he had raised previously. Although the students were ensured the space to respond in journals and in small group discussions, his personal teaching style and way of relating to the students in fact remained largely didactic and authority-centred. It appeared that he was generally accustomed to conducting discussions in an adversarial question-and-answer mode in which the teacher — often quite subconsciously — sets up the perceptual frame of reference through which students are encouraged to view the text.[1] Very rapidly I found my focus widening from students and texts to encompass the teacher himself and his role as a central presence in the classroom.

Furthermore, my hope that the teacher and I would come increasingly to share a deeper level common framework did not actually materialise. Although we began the project with fairly extensive out-of-school discussions and reflections, Alan increasingly withdrew his commitment to these so that by the second term our time was largely reduced to discussing practicalities. It was a period of ever-increasing pressure, with encroachment of the National Curriculum, as well as particular pressures for the project teacher. After serving as Acting Head of Department during the last two terms of the project, he obtained a post of Head of English in another school.

More of the teacher's perspective will emerge in the ensuing chapters but it is perhaps necessary to add that our discussions seemed blocked and constrained at a surface level consideration of racism. Instead of being able to develop what I had hoped would be a genuinely collaborative relationship with the teacher, I found him frequently coming into centre focus of my ethnographic study and feeling myself fundamentally alienated from his way of relating to students. Although some of the original possibilities of the project were thus stunted, I was on the other hand offered access to observing very closely issues of racism and justice being broached in an essentially 'traditional' classroom context by a teacher whose own perspective was limited. Inevitably critical questions were thrown up which need to be addressed in undertaking anti-racist work in white schools.

Raising issues of racism in a white environment is an extremely difficult, uncomfortable area in which to be working and in which one has often to move with considerable sensitivity in attempting to effect change. While as a visiting researcher in St Mary's, I continually put out and drew in my 'feelers' as it were, depending on the responses of others, it is not possible to write an ethnographic study without writing personally. It is not my intention to point any fingers but rather to try to reveal how racism and racist constructions operate, so that we can begin to deconstruct them. I should have greatly preferred to have been able to engage in that process together with the teacher. However, just as I had to adjust to a researcher-teacher relationship which was different from my initial conception, the teacher was no doubt from his perspective faced with a parallel difficulty!

The students and the 'Racist Perceptions Survey'

The selected class formed part of the school's third year 'middle band' (Year 9). It consisted of eighteen boys and twelve girls, aged thirteen to fourteen who had been taught by Alan Parsons in the first year. The students were very conscious of banding. Two boys had been 'promoted' from the lower band and a new boy was 'demoted' early on in the term.

Information I had hoped to receive from the school indicating parental occupations of the project students unfortunately did not materialise. However from informal assessment I gathered that most came within the range of professional, managerial, clerical and skilled manual work. All but one of the thirty students had travelled abroad, either with their families or on school trips, eight of them having visited more than three other countries. This indicates the relative affluence of the area, to which I have already alluded.

At the end of the summer term in 1988, before the course began, a Racist Perceptions Survey I had devised was administered to the entire second year. It was not administered by me personally, in order to prevent a connection being made with the course, and was simply called an 'Opinions Survey'. The students were assured that only the researcher —and not the school — would have access to their completed papers, to preserve anonymity. The survey included one section of quantifiable data. After being asked to complete a number of open-ended sentences about themselves and others, students were asked to respond along a scale of 'agree-disagree' to a list of sixteen statements reflecting perceptions, feelings, values and beliefs relating to issues of 'race'. The same survey was re-administered to the same 177 students sixteen months later, four months after the end of the course when they were in the fourth year.

The purpose of the surveys was mainly to provide a broad, descriptive picture of views held within the project class and within the year-group as a whole, as well as to tap interesting individual responses within the project group which might otherwise not come openly to light in the classroom. Surveys in this field clearly have their limitations and the information derived from them needs to viewed with caution. A fuller description of the survey, the findings and qualifications can be read in the original thesis of the research. The intention, however, was not to provide sophisticated, comparative data but rather the kind of material from which might arise useful insights and questions.

A number of interesting features indeed emerged from the initial survey. The first of these was the existence of a clear gender pattern in response, with girls in the project class tending to cluster towards the lower non-racist end of the scale. While boys scored across the range, fewer were at the non-racist end. Furthermore the project boys' average was skewed by the high racism score of two particular male students. This gender difference in response, with the male average being notably higher than that of female students, was borne out across the year group and tallies with findings and observations of several others (Bagley and Verma 1975; Marsh 1976; Williams 1986, Gaine 1987; Cohen 1987).

A second feature was the apparent discrepancy in a marked number of students between stated value positions against racism (such as asserting

31

equal rights for black and white British children) and behaviour perceived as acceptable (such as racist joking and name-calling). While 90% of the project class agreed with a statement on equal rights and 87% with a statement that racist attitudes needed to be tackled in school, only 43% disagreed that 'Jokes about people from other cultures are just a bit of fun.' Furthermore only 63% were prepared to take an outright position against the use of racist names, by dissenting from the statement that 'Words like paki, wog, chink, gippo are harmless really.' A similar apparent discrepancy was broadly mirrored in responses from the rest of the year group.

A third feature, of particular interest to me in relation to the students I would be observing in the project class, reflected apparent contradictions within an individual set of responses, suggesting the potential complexity within an individual's frame of reference. It seemed possible that within these disjunctures there might be room for perceptual shifts.

Fourthly the initial survey — especially the students' responses in completing open-ended statements — revealed widespread ignorance about black people. Finally there was a notable lack of reference to the socio-historical realities of people's lives. One might well argue that given that the students were only thirteen years old, a lack of socio-historical knowledge was to be expected. I was therefore particularly interested to see if there would be any noticeable change in data from the second survey, when the students would be in their fourth year of secondary schooling. Yet whatever the reasons, if the students were indeed not used to thinking about the socio-historical dimension of people's lives, this would have implications for the project. Although the students would have already experienced literature within the 'personal growth' approach to English teaching (with an emphasis on the individual's linguistic, imaginative and aesthetic development), it seemed likely that the course would be their first introduction to engaging with a 'cultural analysis' view which 'emphasises the role of English in helping children towards a critical understanding of the world and cultural environment in which they live' (DES 1989).

Probably the most notable aspect of the second survey was a fairly widespread increase in average Racist Perceptions scores across the year group. Viewed in this context, while again bearing in mind the limitations of this kind of quantifiable data, the results of the project class appeared to indicate a small movement in the desired direction. While there was a slight increase in the project's male average, it was not as great as that for the rest of the middle and upper band boys in the year group. A small decrease in the girls' average in the project class compared favourably with an average increase for the rest of the middle and upper band girls.

On this basis one might tentatively suggest the course provided some form of deterrent or buffer against a general trend towards an average increase in explicit racism. With a couple of exceptions, including that of girls in the project class, standard deviations in average scores increased across the year in the second survey. This suggested that a number of individual students, in particular males, were expressing more explicit racism than sixteen months previously and that the average score increases might well be largely attributed to rather sharp increases in the scores of certain individuals. This pattern could also be seen amongst a small number of male students in the project class who indeed became more explicitly racist in their views. In contrast, the project girls ended with not only the lowest average racism score of all groups across the year on the Racist Perceptions Survey, but also the lowest standard deviation. In other words, they gave evidence of the greatest degree of consensus.

Although some shifts were observable in individual responses to certain statements on re-administration of the survey, the central features noted previously persisted amongst the project students as in the wider year group. Apart from the continuing gender difference, apparent discrepancies remained in both group and individual frames of reference; there was continued evidence of ignorance and ignoring of black experience; and little reference made to socio-historical knowledge — despite the students now being fifteen to sixteen. Even with students showing strong feelings against racism, it seemed unlikely that for most of them their concept of racism extended much beyond the personal level.

While the survey information on the students remains fairly crude and the project itself clearly limited in its scope to effect major attitudinal change, nevertheless I hope the kind of richness of detail about processes of response that follows in the ensuing chapters will help illuminate some of the complexities in achieving shifts in perception and, beyond that, critical thinking about one's own society.

My role in the classroom

It was agreed that I would be introduced to the students under my non-married name. I was concerned that, if possible, they should not identify my particular interest as a researcher, and I felt that my surname might be a give-away. In addition the school had copies of my book *Journey to Jo'burg*, published under my married name, and we wanted to keep open the option of using the book on the course. Alan therefore introduced me to the students as a researcher who was particularly interested in young people's responses to literature and that I was devising, in collaboration with him, the course and activities they would be following.

For most of the time I sat in one of the front corners of the classroom with a couple of tape-recorders (one as a fail-safe!). The students were aware that I was the main reader of their reading journals as well as 'response sheets' — where they either jotted their thoughts and feelings around the text of a photocopied passage, or perhaps were asked to advise a character or to write someone's thoughts at a particular point. Besides listening to and recording their class discussions, I was also an audience in their small group discussions as nearly all of these were also recorded.

As the project progressed — as can be seen in the outline below — students were able to deduce more of my own perspective and were finally to become aware not only of my specific interest in issues of racism but also of my identity as a writer.

Outline of the course

The course of literature was designed to explore the students' understandings of — and responses to — racism in a variety of contexts and hopefully to challenge racist thinking. Although they were reading and responding to fiction, in discussion they inevitably drew on their perceptions of reality. Underlying links between the different books were not, where possible, openly drawn to their attention so as to see if, and how, the students would make connections themselves.

The sequence in which the books were introduced was important. We started with *Buddy* by Nigel Hinton (1983), where the context was familiar and racism only a side issue. I wanted to be able to observe the students' responses to literature more generally as well as to map their initial levels of awareness of the dimension of racism in the book. The author suggests links between different oppressions with Buddy, a white working class lad whose mother has left home, being befriended by black twins — also outsiders in an otherwise snobbish class where racist jokes are openly condoned by the teacher. The second novel was Hans Peter Richter's *Friedrich* (1978; first German publication 1961), focusing on racism in a European context. The book takes the form of a kind of diary by a non-Jewish boy, charting the rise and fall of his friendship with a Jewish boy in Germany between 1925 and 1942.

From Europe we moved to the American south in the 1930s with Mildred Taylor's *Roll of Thunder, Hear My Cry* (1987; first American publication 1976) where events are seen through the perceptive, indignant and resistant eyes of nine year old Cassie. This was the first class novel the students had read by a black author. It was followed by *Waiting for the Rain* by Sheila Gordon (1987). Set in South Africa, it maps the course of a relationship between Frikkie (nephew of a white farmer) and Tengo (son of the farm's black foreman). The reader is shifted from one characters's consciousness to the other. Tengo's growth in awareness of himself and his position leads to a final confrontation between the two as young men. The book's strength is that racism is located in the structure of social relationships, revealing that it is more than personal prejudice. This is also the case in *Friedrich* and *Roll of Thunder, Hear My Cry* and I was particularly interested to know whether any students would be able to perceive this.

My original intention was to complete the course with literature which focused on racism in a British context, for instance through a number of short stories. On realising, however, that we were running out of time, I arranged for the students to see the BBC series *Getting to Grips with Racism*

(BBC 1988) during Religious Education time in the final term. A senior teacher who had attended a DES Multicultural Education course agreed to lead these sessions. This brought the students' discussions of racism out of the arena of understanding literature and human relationships in general —and very directly into the arena of considering themselves and their society. I was present during these sessions, which meant that the students were thereafter able to identify my interest as very obviously extending beyond their responses to literature. In addition, during this period, the class learnt of my married name and of my identity as a writer.

Throughout the course attempts were made to provide students with some knowledge of context where this was unfamiliar. For instance, they viewed a number of videos relating to a number of the texts and listened to various author interviews. Apart from certain additional background material being provided for everyone, students were able to borrow books (mainly fiction) for personal reading from a specially selected loan collection. They were also at times engaged in related activities, for example deconstructing two versions of South African history in connection with *Waiting for the Rain.*

In addition to a number of lessons being spent on inter-related poetry, drama sessions over the year were linked to issues arising in the literature, although not always overtly. Themes included victimisation through 'jokes'; child/ adult conflicts; status and power in teacher/parent relationships; personal experiences of injustice; inter-school rivalry related to status, power and prejudice; master/slave relationships; emigration from the Caribbean to the 'Motherland'; arrival in a new country and encounters with racist behaviour. The drama method of 'hotseating' — involving volunteers answering questions in role — was used directly in connection with the literature.

Visitors were a significant element of the course in terms of the intention to challenge perspectives. The writer Millie Murray agreed to be hotseated as the black twin Charmian from *Buddy,* ten years on, and then as Charmian's mother — switching from London to Jamaican English. Later Millie returned to be hotseated as Cassie, Cassie's mother and grandmother in *Roll of Thunder, Hear My Cry.*

The class was involved in commemorating the fiftieth anniversary of *Kristallnacht* —which occurred during the reading of *Friedrich* — with a visit from an elderly Jewish couple who had escaped from Vienna a few months after the Nazi invasion. Drama director Richard Finch devised two workshops for the students relating to Nazi persecution; the first on the theme of 'the outsider' and the second on survival. The latter was accompanied by a visit to the Anne Frank exhibition.

A science session by two teachers, one black and one white — Mike Vance and John Siraj-Blatchford — was designed to raise questions about classification and the notion of 'race', as an introduction to the South African novel. The Caribbean writer James Berry performed and spoke about some of his poems which, as he says, 'reflect two cultures' (1988) — sometimes distinct, sometimes merging. His visit took place at the time the students were experiencing drama involving issues of migration, as well as viewing the *Getting to Grips with Racism* (BBC 1988) programme on immigration.

In the final 'Media Week', dramatist/director Olusola Oyeleye led the students during five afternoon workshops in which they met a variety of people concerned with racism in their working lives. The intention was that the students develop their own ideas on what should go into a TV programme about racism for young people in a largely white area like their own. The week included interviews, role playing, discussions and improvisations, the latter being videoed and discussed on the final day with Peter Evans, BBC producer of *Getting to Grips with Racism.*

Finally the project ended with a variety of evaluations, including one with the students by Chris Gaine. Given the extensive nature of the course, as mentioned previously, I have necessarily had to be selective in the following chapters, focusing on what seemed to me to be some of the key issues over the year.

Notes to Chapter 2

1   This derives from a method of literature teaching based upon what Michael Benton (1988) refers to as 'the conventional, inherited ideas of comprehension and criticism which, in the absence of anything else, have passed for the conceptual bases'.

Chapter Three

Initial explorations into racism in a local fictional context — responses to Buddy

Outline of *'Buddy'* and related activities

The central theme in Nigel Hinton's novel is that of an English teenager's difficulty in accepting the break-up of his parents' marriage. In a desperate move to establish a life for herself, Buddy's mother leaves her thirteen-year-old son and husband Terry, a Buddy Holly fanatic who appears to live on fantasy. Buddy is left to cope with his errant 'Teddy Boy' father who already has one jail term behind him. In addition, although Buddy is white like the majority of students in the 'Express' class at school, he is isolated through being working class and obviously poor. His only real friends are two resilient black twins, Charmian and Julius Rybeero, isolated through racism.

The novel contains a range of themes and the extracts selected for specific responses focused on Buddy's relationships with his peers, his mother and his father, as well as touching on racism. When students hotseated each other in role — and subsequently the writer Millie Murray as Charmian and Mrs Rybeero — racism formed only part of a much wider canvas of concerns.

In order to allow exploration of the students' sense of themselves as young people and potential feelings of constriction, the students were introduced to a slightly truncated version of James Berry's poem 'Dreaming Black Boy' (1988). It was re-titled 'I Wish' in order to gather their responses (jottings around the text and small group discussions) without having identified for them the fact that the poet, or the central young voice in the poem, was black. In the following lesson however, after hearing a short interview with James Berry in which he spoke about why he had written the poem and how he had drawn on his own experiences as a black person, they were then asked to respond to the same poem again. Students also wrote and discussed their own 'I Wish' poems.

In drama the focus was on their own experiences of being victims of 'jokes', followed by conflicts or differences in outlook between adults and children. The rationale behind the drama as well as the poetry activities was that it was important to start the project with the students being able to explore some of their own perspectives, interests and entitlements as young people.

Given these intentions, *Buddy* provided a useful starting off point for the whole course, proving a popular choice with nearly all the students. It also enabled me to gather an idea of the ways in which the students approached both reading and responding in a journal before the introduction of the novels more specifically related to themes such as inequality, injustice and racism. I also wanted to see whether students would be sensitive to the issues of racism within *Buddy* or whether they would tend to pass them over as not being central to the story.

Responses surrounding the racist joke incident

The first passage to which students were asked to respond provided a particularly good opportunity for this. In it Buddy compromises himself by joining in 'the general chuckle' with the Express class at a racist joke directed at his two absent friends. The joke is condoned by the teacher Mr Normington, and Buddy, instead of openly defending the twins, or at least not participating, submits to his desire 'to belong'. He hates himself for the betrayal and sees his later humiliation by the teacher as his punishment. I was particularly interested in how students would respond to this incident in view of only 43% of the class in the first survey having categorically rejected the statement that 'Jokes about people from other cultures are just a bit of fun'. Apart from responding individually in writing to the extract, the students discussed the first two chapters of the book in groups. They were encouraged to note in their reading journals any shifts or reinforcement of their views after the discussion.

Some questions of gender

While most students made some reference to racism and nine of them — all girls — expressed personal disapproval, only three students (John, Terry and Michael) made no reference in their writing to any element of racism, or even simply to colour. All three were above average in expressing racist views as judged on the first Racist Perceptions Survey, with John being the highest scorer in the class. I was particularly interested in Michael's responses as he struck me as a sensitive boy, without some of the male bravado that seemed to be a dimension of both John and Terry's behaviour. In his discussion group (Michael, Marco, Marion, Caroline), Michael focused on

Buddy's poverty and his maltreatment by a class of 'snobby children' who were 'cruel' to Buddy (in the litter incident) as well as on Buddy's need for his mum, including her income ('I mean a boy can't survive without his mother you know'). Neither he nor Marco followed up statements contributed by both the girls in their group, Marion and Caroline, condemning the racism and the teacher's complicity:

> MARION: I feel strongly about the way the teacher was letting all the racist remarks about the twins happen and the way Buddy was feeling left out and all he could do was laugh instead of acting like he was their friends.

> MARCO: Right and now we can go on to the next person in our group...

> ...

> CAROLINE: I think that instead of the teacher joining in on the joke of the coloured boys and the fruit stall I think he should have told the children off about it.

> MARCO: That's right. Thank you very much Caroline and now we go on with a social discussion where we can hear everyone discussing very clearly...

Transcription conventions used throughout text:
.. indicates brief hesitation or pause by speaker
... indicates speech omitted from transcription
- indicates speaker is cut-off by next speaker

This was the students' first experience of group discussions in the year and I gathered it had not been a customary procedure within English classes for them, certainly not with the additional use of a tape recorder. In this group Marco, acting rather like a compere, controlled the microphone and his responses seem to have been somewhat conditioned by the novelty of the situation. However, on both occasions when the girls referred to racism he moved the discussion elsewhere. His own response seemed to be largely focused on the social class difference between Buddy and the majority, although he didn't go beyond expressing personal distaste that 'it was a very high social class and I don't think he (Buddy) belongs there'. While Marco was amongst those showing the lowest degree of racist perceptions on the first survey, he seemed satisfied here by predicting that Buddy would one day get his revenge on the 'horrible' Mr Normington. One can only speculate on how much Marco was maintaining a low profile in terms of his own response to the specific racist elements at this point. Over the year it became apparent that his understanding of racism was linked to his own ethnic minority experience as an Italian and that he had generally adopted a strategy of assimilation. The net effect in the discussion, however, was that the girls' criticism of the racism in the classroom incident was lost.

A similar gender pattern emerged in Terry's group (Alison, Julia, Louise, Terry, Greg). Once again the focus on racism was initiated, and indeed sustained for a short while, by girls in the group. While Terry's friend Greg (also with a medium high score on the first Racist Perceptions Survey) appeared to reinforce disapproval of the twins being picked on because of their colour, Terry switched the conversation onto Buddy's isolation because the class were 'a bunch of snobs'. Like Marco, he wanted Buddy to 'get his revenge'. In this group the girls were rather more effective than in the previous group in holding on to their responses to the racism. However when Julia and Louise declared they would have 'stood up to them (the class) and told them it wasn't funny', Terry completely re-focused the discussion onto a justification of Buddy's theft of the five pounds from his mum. Here he was directly challenged by Louise ('...but it's still thieving') and quickly gave way, although probably at lip-service level only. It seems likely that the balance of three girls to two boys in this group influenced its dynamics, giving the girls more confidence. All three girls in this group rarely spoke in class discussions despite expressing themselves strongly at times in their reading journals.

Sympathy for Buddy's isolation
Throughout all the discussions, there seemed to be considerable sympathy for Buddy's isolation. John saw Buddy's isolation as responsible for his friendship with the Rybeero twins. It seems he found it necessary to justify a white-black friendship:

> GRAHAM: Why do you think the black people were the only people that he knew and liked?

> TONY: It was really that they were his own type of people. He could chat to them and they had been friends ever since.

> JOHN: I think um the black people were his friends because they were um.. Buddy didn't really get on in the class and neither did they. That's why I think that um he made friends with the black people.

John also used fear of isolation as justification for participation in a racist joke. When Donald, the fourth member of this group, strongly condemned the behaviour of the class and its teacher ('I hate people that make jokes about blacks'), John did not challenge this openly. Instead he opened up room for query:

> JOHN: Would you have laughed though when he made the joke 'cause if you hadn't laughed wouldn't you have felt a bit out of.. you know—

DONALD (emphatically): No! um I don't..this is a full stop. I mean I hate people that make jokes about blacks...

GRAHAM: But even if you were one of the children not Buddy but one of the children in the class wouldn't you have laughed?

Not surprisingly, both John and Graham had agreed with the survey statement that 'Jokes about people from other cultures are just a bit of fun.' Despite his emphatic response and general doggedness, Donald was open to confusion and an easy butt himself for jokes. His tendency to contradict himself was revealed on the first page of his journal where he repeated his statement against racist jokes a few lines after having referred to Chinese food as 'chinky' (commenting on the front picture showing Buddy and his father with 'take-away' food).

The consequences of not joining in the joke were taken up in another group where the conversation was almost totally dominated by the boys (Philip, Andrew, Simon, Jacky, Gaby). Simon began by raising the question:

SIMON: I know it's not very kind to laugh at it but if you hadn't you probably would have been embarrassed if you hadn't have laughed.

By the end of the discussion, after Philip had declared how 'really cruel' the joke was — and had gone further to say he probably would not have laughed — Simon seemed even clearer about his position:

SIMON: I would have laughed like um I must admit I wouldn't have just stood there and not laughed because it would have been embarrassing for him as well.

Writing in his journal after the discussion Simon noted that his own focus seemed to be more on Buddy's feelings 'while the rest of the group were talking about the coloured twins joke'. Although he noted this difference in perspective, there was no indication that his own had shifted.

'You just don't get racist teachers'

An area of common agreement across the class, however, was reflected in widespread criticism of the teacher. In discussion and writing, a couple of students even queried whether a teacher would actually behave in as racist a manner as Mr Normington. For instance the following student, Paul, reveals considerable confidence in the teaching profession:

PAUL: No teachers would be racist. I mean they would know better. I know it's just a story but I mean, you just don't get racist teachers.

Although a couple of students indicated that Mr Normington reminded them of a teacher they had come across, it appeared that most students at St Mary's generally expected authority to uphold certain values, including fairness and justice. A couple of students in fact referred to Mr Normington as having 'stooped down' to the level of the children.

Contrasts: Angela and Ian

The most rigorous of the taped discussions on this occasion took place amongst the group including Angela, the Irish-born student who from the first had stood out as the only girl who did not hold back in whole class discussions. Although the group had three girls to two boys (Angela, Tanya, Erica, Ian, Neil), Angela would most likely have held her own in any group, her contribution clearly being the most dominant.

The discussion was distinguished by the students not only offering their own affective responses to the racism and class prejudice but exploring to some extent how they worked, as well as making connections with their own experiences in a banded school. This analytical approach was largely led by Angela. Whereas some students in other groups had spoken about the majority of the Express stream children as 'snobby' or 'posh', no one had moved much beyond expressing personal repulsion. The opening dialogue of this group indicates Angela's strong influence as well as some pointed contributions from others:

> ANGELA: I think my strongest point of what I found in there was the insulting one about the fruit shop.. the joke that they played.

> NEIL: Yeah, and the fact that the teacher joined in it as well meaning that he's setting a bad example.

> IAN: I think he should really stop the class from having jibes at the person instead of joining in himself.

> TANYA: Yeah, especially the racist jokes.

> NEIL: And when they are not there either, which is even worse.

> TANYA: I've never met a teacher like that, never met a teacher who has said that.

> ANGELA: I have! I won't tell you who (giggles).. I think it's really bad.

> ERICA: I think if I was Buddy in that situation I would have laughed as well not to be left out of the class—

> ANGELA: I wouldn't.

> ERICA: ..and not to be left out of the joke.

> TANYA/NEIL?: No I wouldn't.

ANGELA: If they're his strongest friends and they stick up for him when they're there even though there are two of them um I would stick up for them.

ERICA: Yeah I know but if you hadn't you see everybody would have started picking on you and saying—

TANYA?: They pick on him anyway don't they?

ANGELA: Yeah but it's your belief isn't it really? They're upper class they are bound to pick on him anyway because he's only working class.

ERICA: O.K.

(Pause and whispering)

IAN: I think another point is the thing that struck me most was he wished the twins weren't away because if you are in a classroom on your own you get very lonely especially with people taking the micky out of you.

With Angela so forthright, it's difficult to know whether Erica had indeed changed her position when she said 'O.K.' or was simply wanting to deflect the conversation. Ian (the second highest scorer on the first Racist Perceptions Survey and who later revealed himself to be the class's most adept racist joker) not only steered clear of confronting Angela but joined in by focusing on the teacher 'having jibes at the person' without being specific about the nature of those jibes. Interestingly, after the brief pause, he re-focused the discussion on Buddy's sense of isolation, quickly slipping into the closer pronoun 'you' when speaking about being lonely and 'people taking the micky out of you'.

As in responses elsewhere, Ian revealed here his own identification with feelings of isolation. However evidence of how his racist frame of reference set parameters to this identification was strongly reflected in his sequence of responses to James Berry's poem 'Dreaming Black Boy'. On the first occasion, when it was presented to the students entitled 'I Wish' without any information on the identity of the poet and voice within the poem, Ian revealed intense empathy with the sense of being put down. On responding a second time with the knowledge that the central voice was that of a black child, he distanced himself, making no first-person statements and restricted himself to third person commentary. It is a matter of conjecture how conscious Ian was of covering up his real feelings from the rest of the group in this discussion, given the general disapproval of the racism. His journal comment on the text at this point suggests a possible strategy of giving what he thought would be 'appropriate'.

'It is very good also of the reason he (Buddy) has grown to like two people of a different race and colour. It shows that either your home

43

background has made no favours by discuraging friends or you are placed with people which you think are SNOBS'.

His very formulation, however, indicates that he holds deep constructs of 'racial' difference, finding it necessary for instance to explain how people of 'a different race and colour' could in fact be friends. While the second survey indicated that Ian's racist frame of reference indeed became more entrenched by the end of the project, there was evidence in the course of the year of him not only using racist joking as a means of asserting his own perceptions and undermining possible anti-racist consensus, but also of him becoming more explicit in his views.

Returning to the conversation quoted above, one can see a strong interplay of affective and cognitive responses. Angela's initial personal response to the 'insulting' joke was followed immediately by Neil's identification of the teacher's role in perpetuating the insult by 'setting a bad example' and Tanya's pointed comment that the insult had special significance because it was racist. After some of the group had stated how they thought they would have behaved if in a similar position to Buddy's, Angela attempted to see the pattern in what had happened. It was a matter of 'belief' and of fundamental class hierarchy. Her confident tone suggests terms such as 'upper class' and 'working class' were familiar constructs, to which she had quite possibly been introduced at home. Certainly she seemed to bring to the discussion a level of analysis not evident in the other groups. A further example of this ability to analyse was reflected in Angela's reference to the author and his construction of the character Buddy. It was this line of thinking that probably led Tanya to making an important observation about the presence of black characters in the book:

> ANGELA: ...a point that struck me was how desperate the author makes Buddy.. makes the character Buddy feel for change in his life which given his background is understandable because everybody else has probably got you know their own parents and they live in a big house and they get lifts to school and pocket money and all that lot and he doesn't.

> IAN: I think if they understood his problem I think they would never treat him as they treat him now.

> ANGELA: Exactly.

> (Pause)

> TANYA: It's a good point that the author mentioned the black.. the black kids.

> ANGELA: Yeah but you don't usually get that in a lot of books.

> TANYA: No, no.

ANGELA: I think that's a good point.

TANYA: And all the snide remarks.

ANGELA: Another point you know the Express classes.. you know he's always talking about all the standards and everything. That reminds me of this school...

Tanya's reference to black characters was an interesting development of a comment she had previously made in her passage-response sheet. In relation to a sentence about Buddy never having had black friends before, she had written:

'I think that's a good point to make. The way that the word 'Black' is used instead of 'coloured'. I have had black mates before and they don't like being called 'coloured' they wouldn't mind so much being called Nigros than coloured'.

It was unfortunate that I did not pick out this comment at the time and suggest a way of using it to raise the consciousness of the other students regarding terminology. It should have been possible to have embedded such a discussion within a framework of dealing with issues raised by the students themselves, rather than it being identified as a focus of specific teacher-concern. The heavy programme and constraints of time unfortunately did not always allow sufficient time for feed-back and reflection on student responses. Alternatively, had the teacher been more amenable to links between lessons set aside for 'language work' and the literature course, exploration of this kind of issue would have had a natural place in terms of 'knowledge about language'. As it was, despite the term 'black' being used by the teacher and all the visitors to the project, as well as in the literature itself, some of the students (including those with low scores on the Racist Perceptions Survey) continued to use the term 'coloured'. Some students used both terms, including on occasions even Tanya.

Angela can be seen, at the end of this last transcript extract, yet again moving the discussion on, into consideration of some of the effects of banding in their own school. It is worth noting that Angela, like many other students, was incorporating points she had made in her passage-response sheet into the discussion, where she was able to share and expand them. In other words, the methodology provided space for students to develop and reflect on personal responses.

A final point about Angela's contribution was that she was the only student to place an explicitly positive focus on the black characters at this stage, not simply perceiving them passively as friends of Buddy's or as victims of racism. Instead, when referring to Buddy's humiliating treatment by the teacher and class, she noted how 'The twins give him courage to take it lightly and help him carry on.' While a few students in their passage-response sheets focused on 'the spiteful jibes' experienced by the twins,

45

Angela was the only person to underline the whole phrase about Buddy's admiration for 'the cheerful way they ignored all the spiteful jibes'. Possibly their positive resilience was something to which she could relate in terms of her own experience of finding ways of responding to anti-Irish jibes. Angela's responses come under closer scrutiny, with some contradictions surfacing later through a rather revealing role play and hotseating session (Chapter 7, p.107/8) and in an inadvertently tape-recorded racist joking session led by Ian, in which Angela offered an anti-Irish joke to the repertoire.

Given that Buddy as a character elicits considerable sympathy from readers and that the twins are portrayed as cheerful, supportive and friendly towards him, it would have been surprising had any of the students shown actual antipathy towards them. They are essentially assimilable by white readers, including those holding more entrenched racist frames of reference. It is common to hear of people who articulate racist stereotypes, at the same time claiming that a friend of theirs, who potentially fits into their stereotyped group, is not included — 'Oh I'm not talking about 'x'... he's different, he's my mate!' Julius and Charmian could easily be seen as special exceptions. For instance, Ian wrote in his journal:

> 'The twins seem to come down to earth with Buddy and do what most people would do together. They are treated differently by the class but just one of the guys by Buddy. They seem to get stronger each day'.

There seems to be a sense of surprise in Ian's formulation that the twins 'would do what most people would do together'. Why otherwise would he mention it? His perspective was in marked contrast with that of Alison, who seemed to be trying to express the idea of equality without denial of difference — in other words the opposite of assimilation:

> 'I like the way that Julius and Charmian treat him (Buddy) they treat him like they have no differences but they don't really take away the colour'.

Responses to Buddy at the Satellite Club: 'one of the few whites'

For most of the book, the twins being black does not present a challenge either to Buddy or to the reader. The few exceptions to this include the racist joking incident and when Buddy's father makes racist comments about the twins' family. But perhaps the sharpest, albeit brief, challenge occurs in Chapter Five when Buddy visits the Satellite Club, a youth club attended mainly by young black people. The author notes that Buddy's strategy is to arrive late so that Julius and Charmian would already be there as 'he still felt a bit awkward about being one of the few whites among so many blacks.' The tension is sharpened by the author introducing a black friend of Julius' called Dennis whose attitude towards Buddy is clearly one of hostility.

Buddy is unsettled because 'The boy's eyes had been filled with hatred'. Julius attempts to set Buddy at ease by telling him not to worry about Dennis:

> 'Hey, you play ok,' Julius said, coming up to him at the end. Buddy shrugged but he felt like smiling. 'Where's that other bloke?' 'Oh, Dennis — he's gone. Don't mind him — he had a bit of bother from some white kids at his school today.' 'So did I,' Buddy said. 'Yeah — yeah I should've told him that. Not the same, though.' 'Why not?' 'Just isn't,' Julius said vaguely and then groaned. 'Oh no — it's the Minister...'

While the author does not explore Julius' point that the trouble experienced by Dennis is not the same as that undergone by Buddy, the incident nevertheless provides a good opening to discuss the issues. For example, what makes racist name-calling different from other name-calling when each is personally hurtful to the recipient? After reading Chapter Five, the students were asked to write their immediate responses in their journals which was then followed by a class discussion. The latter unfortunately provided an example of how the potential to deepen students' understanding may well be blocked, albeit unwittingly, by a teacher using too didactic a methodology combined with too narrow a conception of racism.

An analysis of the transcript also revealed notable differences in the extent of male/female involvement, with 44% of the boys speaking more than once compared with only 16% of the girls. In other words, boys proportionately offered well over twice as many contributions as girls. This lack of participation by girls in whole class discussions was to be a feature throughout the year, raising questions not only about teaching style and gender bias in general, but also having implications for teaching about 'race' in particular. I have already indicated earlier in the chapter how within small mixed-group discussions it was the girls who raised the issues of racism. This is an issue to which I shall return.

Conceptions of racism and the quest for moral 'balance'

In the class discussion about the Satellite Youth Club, the direction and parameters were very significantly set by a tightly teacher-controlled question-and-answer format. His questions would also have been influenced by what he perceived as my particular focus, without our actually having come to a consensus in our understanding of racism. It should also be remembered that he was having to respond quickly 'on his feet'.

Following an initial question from the teacher about how Buddy had reacted to entering the Satellite Club, Paul related his own feelings of uneasiness when entering a Youth Club. A further probe by Alan led to two students raising the black/white dimension from their white perspective. While Graham spoke about the Satellite Youth Club being a 'very very strange environment' and that it would have been easier for Buddy to go into a white Youth Club, John openly acknowledged:

> If it was me I don't think I would have even tried to go in there... I'd feel too out of place and all these black people looking at you and people staring--- [inaudible] I'd be frightened what to say.

The only person to contest this openly was Donald, with the explicit value statement 'I don't believe you know I don't think there's any difference between whites and blacks apart from their colour'. He was immediately challenged by Graham to recognise that there were people who thought differently. However an intervention from the teacher moved the focus back to the text with a question about 'What makes it awkward...?' for Buddy. Rather than encouraging any perception of the wider social situation which underlies black and white youth attending largely separate youth clubs in the first place, the answer the teacher was clearly seeking was identification of the black boy Dennis as the factor making 'it awkward' for Buddy. Alan Parsons thereafter sustained the focus on Dennis and his hostility to Buddy for the rest of the discussion. After eliciting that there had been 'hatred' in Dennis' eyes, Alan further reinforced it with his question 'Did that strike you that word?':

A.P.: What does it actually state in the text.. that's in his eyes?

VOICES: Hatred.

A.P.: Did that strike you that word?

VOICES: Yeah.

A.P.: How does Julius account for that?... Marion?

MARION: He'd had some trouble with some white kids at school.

A.P.: He'd had some trouble with some white kids at school.. and how does Buddy reply to that? It's quite a sharp reply actually.. Neil?

NEIL: So did I.

A.P.: So did I. Will Julius accept the parallel?   (Murmurs 'No'. Long pause)

...

IAN: Julius will but his friends won't.

By adding 'It's quite a sharp reply actually', the teacher was prematurely endorsing Buddy's perception that his own trouble at school was the equivalent to that of Dennis, before the students had explored the issue themselves. It is not possible to deduce whether the long pause was the result of difficulty with the way the question had been phrased in an abstract way (a tendency of Alan's) or whether the pause was indicative of a problem in formulating their own responses. Ian's reply indicates his desire to separate out Julius, a character he could assimilate, from Julius' black friends — undefined and presumably threatening.

A few reading journal responses indicated strong sympathy for Buddy's point, for instance:

> '...the boy talking to Julius had a bad time in school with white kids and took it out on Buddy just because he's white it doesn't mean to say everybody's the same as that.' (Louise)

> 'Julius' friend Dennis shouldn't have judged Buddy by his appearance just because he was white and Dennis had got hassle from some white kids. Buddy was feeling awkward going into that youth club I don't think I would but other people probably would... I don't see why Buddy's sort of hassling was different to Dennis' I mean they were both hassled about there appearance from white kids.' (Alison)

These responses, both from girls with low Racist Perceptions scores, indicate a lack of understanding of the power dimension to racism and the fact that it is a life-long ongoing experience, as well as the limitations of perceiving racism purely as being about attitudes on a personal level. This indeed appeared to be part of the teacher's frame of reference as well, preventing him from seeing what the tenacious student Philip was getting at by distinguishing a difference in white and black name-calling. Instead of being able to help clarify the broader social implications, Alan Parsons' response actually blocked Philip's line of enquiry:

> PHILIP: Well it's not so bad you know say if I have trouble with a white but if blacks have trouble with whites and whites have trouble with blacks it's different... if a black has trouble with whites there's all different names that white people call blacks.

> A.P.: Somebody could name names that white kids call white kids!

> PHILIP: Yeah, but you can't call names that white kids call black kids you can't call a white kid that.

The distinction which Philip was trying to make was one which needed to be explored further in order for students to discover how racist name-calling fits into a wider network of racism and discrimination through the society. They needed to consider how there would have been the possibility at least of a change in the circumstances and features which led to Buddy being called 'Dustman'. This would not have been the case for Dennis. He would still remain black and subject to racism. While the students might still have retained their sympathy for Buddy in feeling himself an unfair personal target for Dennis' hostility, they needed also to develop an understanding of Dennis' position and some conception of structural racism. Instead

49

however, the teacher blocked discussion on the issue, reinforcing a narrow focus on Dennis at a personal level by insisting on the question 'What's your attitude towards Dennis...?' Marion and Jacky both offered replies which continued to be concerned with the process behind Dennis' response:

> MARION: Him being black. He thought it was I suppose being racist but when the white kids have an argument they wouldn't think that---
>
> A.P.: Jacky?
>
> JACKY: He kind of thinks that all white kids will be against him as well.
>
> A.P.: Yes, but I was actually asking more directly what's your attitude towards the character Dennis.
>
> JACKY: He kind of thinks that the white kids are the same.
>
> A.P.: No, I'll ask again. What's your attitude towards Dennis... Ian?
>
> IAN: Well he's sort of a typical black because they sort of judge you as how they judge their friends and you're a different colour and they think that you make racialist remarks about them whatever. They think you're in a sort of gang, who sort of make remarks about them.
>
> A.P.: So you don't like him?
>
> IAN: No.
>
> A.P.: Not sympathetic towards him.

While Marion and Jacky's responses were brushed aside, Alan Parsons' question was finally answered by Ian in an explicitly racist and revealing statement. However the teacher made no attempt to elicit any qualification on this response to Dennis, but instead set up the loaded question 'Isn't he doing exactly what 3E is doing?' At this point Brian, a new boy who had come from London to the school but who was soon afterwards demoted to the lower band, offered the explanation:

> BRIAN: He's probably doing that to Buddy because he's had trouble with white people in the past... He's probably saying he can't trust white people--- [inaudible]

By this time the bell had rung and there was no time to explore Brian's perceptions. It seems unlikely, however, that even if there had been time that the teacher would have followed this route. His final question once again implied that he saw an equation between the racist 3E's behaviour and that of Dennis. In other words, he held a notion of moral balance in which racism and reaction to racism were completely personalised and equated as equally bad.

This marginalising of the broader context of fundamental racist inequality is widespread in the dominant white community. As will be seen in subsequent chapters, the teacher's own narrow construction of racism remained a significant feature over the year. While this clearly placed limitations on broadening the students' conceptions of racism and also affected their perception of black people whose critique and responses were perceived as 'too extreme', it was nevertheless still possible to work within a framework of challenging racism at a personal level — in particular challenging certain stereotypes. A hotseating session, in which students undertook to be questioned in role as various characters from the novel, underlined the need for this in relation to the black characters. This led to setting up a session with the writer Millie Murray in role as Charmian and her mother. This process of challenging stereotypes in which Millie engaged with the students is described in Chapter Seven on 'Approaches through Drama'.

Finally, it is important to note that through their own engagement with the text, students were beginning to make points pertinent to black/white relationships — such as those quoted by Philip, Marion, Jacky, Brian — which a teacher with a deeper conception of racism could well have, in turn, helped to develop. Thus although racism is not a central focus in *Buddy,* certain 'gaps' in the narrative not only invite exploration but offer a framework for extending students' understandings.

Chapter Four

Moral dilemmas in a European historical context — responses to Friedrich

Outline of *Friedrich* and related activities

This novel, translated from German, is the first in a trilogy covering the years of the Third Reich. Written in the first person by Hans Peter Richter who was himself in the Nazi Youth, *Friedrich* is the story of the non-Jewish narrator's relationship with a Jewish boy. The book charts events in the lives of the two boys, born within a week of each other into German families living as tenants in the same house. In the early years Friedrich's Jewish family — the Schneiders — are comparatively well off, while the narrator's father is unemployed — but all that is soon reversed. The story is a powerful one of group pressure, fear and terror in which the narrator's ordinarily decent family are increasingly compromised. With the narrator's account in semidiary form, the book contains a strong interplay of fiction and reality.

The major difference for students approaching *Friedrich* in contrast to *Buddy* was their lack of knowledge of the context out of which the novel arose. Both in terms of time and place it was out of their experience. Nor had they studied the rise of fascism in history. The English Programme video on *Friedrich* (1984), which included documentary footage as well as interviews with people recalling similar experiences to those in the novel, was therefore an important resource.

Apart from their journal writing, the students were asked to respond to a number of specific passages and specially prepared sheets, while the term's poetry and drama also related to themes within the novel. Drama director Richard Finch explored the concepts of 'the outsider' and 'survival' with students in two workshops, the second linked to a visit to the Anne Frank Exhibition. The students also viewed a couple of videos focusing on the experience of young people, including the powerful *Through Our Eyes — Children Witness The Holocaust* (Tatelbaum 1985). Perhaps the most important means of 'bringing it home' however was a commemoration of the 50th anniversary of the *Kristallnacht* pogrom (10th November 1938) with a visit and talk by an elderly Jewish couple who had escaped from Vienna with their two children a couple of months after the Nazi invasion.

Commemoration of *Kristallnacht*: living history

While assessing the impact of these various inputs is extremely difficult, in particular any long-term impact, my own feeling was that the commemoration visit was of an emotional quality not to be easily forgotten. It appeared from journal comments that the visitors brought the book alive in a profound way for some students. For instance, Alison's initial response was that the book 'doesn't look very intresting... if I saw this book in a shop window I doubt I'd go in and buy it.' After the first three chapters she still wrote 'nothing wants to make me read on.' Her next entry however reflects her response to the visitors:

> 'At first I thought it would be boring and I'd probably fall asleep, but I found it very intresting... There were some questions that Mrs Engel didn't want to discuss maybe because they bought back bad memories, others she gave very short answers to, or rushed her husband on not because they wanted to answer as many questions as they could, but because it was probably a personal thing or a subject to close to her heart. They got emotional and their answers moved me deeply... I've changed my mind about the book especially when we heard what Dr Engel and his wife had to say.'

Moral dilemmas: what to do about the Rabbi?

Questions of individual responsibility underpin the book and were central to many of the passages to which the students were asked to respond. In some of the passages I was interested to see if, and how, students would comment on the implicit moral issues, relating for instance to the anti-semitism of the narrator's grandfather and to the boycott of Jewish shops. However in the passage drawn from 'The Rabbi', I decided to direct the students' focus far more explicitly and sharply. In this chapter, three years after the death of Friedrich's mother in the pogrom, Friedrich and his father are continuing to eke out their threatened existence when the narrator discovers an elderly Rabbi hiding with them. The old man declares that his fate lies in the young narrator's hands. The students were asked on their response sheets to advise the narrator and after completing these they discussed the issues in small groups. I was not interested simply in their final decisions as hypothetical advisers to the narrator, but more in the basis on which they arrived at that position — the values, assumptions and perceptions underlying their judgement.

As could be expected, few students found the decision clear-cut. Many presented arguments in both directions before deciding on their advice. In their written responses a third leant towards giving the rabbi up to the authorities, with varying degrees of compunction, while more than half of the class leant towards advising the narrator not to report the rabbi. A number of the latter however changed positions during the group discussions. The major deterrent against informing on the rabbi appeared to be a strong feeling about living with guilt. Expressing considerable conflict, Peter nevertheless wrote: 'I would never forgive myself if they were all tortured.' Like Peter, Angela placed herself directly in the narrator's position, spelling out her dilemma clearly:

> 'My feelings towards such a desicion would be very mixed, because even though I would not know the Rabbi I would have to put myself in his position to see his point of view. Then, what about myself, my parents I would be endangering them to save a stranger who might get caught anyway. I wouldn't know what to do but I'd probably make a rash desicion and wait for the outcome. Would I regret it, can I trust these people? Yes, thinking now I would probably let the Rabbi stay, all our lives would be in danger but I would know that if I died I would die knowing that I might of helped save the life of another man. '

While counterposing saving a stranger with endangering her own family, Angela nevertheless considered it fundamental 'to put myself in his position to see his point of view'. This suggests belief in an intrinsic equality amongst human beings — that even a stranger was entitled to have his point of view considered. Within this frame of reference, her own family appeared not to have an automatic right to survive at the expense of others. She reconciled herself to things going wrong through re-affirming the value of saving another human being's life. This sentiment was closely echoed by Caroline. Turning the rabbi away would induce 'deep guilt', while the compensation for being caught protecting the rabbi would be the knowledge of having 'helped and saved someone'. Nevertheless Caroline commented that 'the rabbi is putting a great burden on the narrator'.

While Alison appeared to feel some resentment towards the rabbi for 'causing a lot of trouble' and for putting the narrator 'in a very awkward situation, pressurising him', she too expressed the rabbi's entitlement as a fellow human being:

> 'The Rabbi might be a stranger, but that wouldn't give me the right to throw him out into a country where he will suffer.'

She was conscious too that the narrator was 'a bit young to tell an old man to get out of a place he doesn't even own'. In other words, her belief in a fundamental respect of youth for age appeared to take precedence over the narrator using his potential power as Gentile over Jew. However Alison still sought a solution in which the danger was removed elsewhere:

> 'If the narrator said nothing that would be causing danger for everyone including himself... I would tell the Rabbi politely that he is dangering many lives, and ask wether he has other friends he can stay with.'

Alison's criticism that the rabbi was 'pressurising' the narrator suggests she did not fully grasp the extent to which the rabbi himself was a victim, and not a willing agent, of pressure. This was certainly the case with Gaby's response. While conscience dictated the rabbi should be helped, Gaby felt

> 'the Rabbi should have not given the narrator such a task or given him an ultimate decision... My feelings would maybe sometimes be of hatred towards the Rabbi to do such a thing and also of bravery of having saved somebody's life through a promise.'

The rabbi appeared to have become the scapegoat for an anger more appropriately directed at the Nazi instigators of the terror. In discussion both Gaby and her friend Jacky revised their written decisions not to inform on the rabbi. Following Jacky's assertion that the Nazis were bound to find them and 'so it might be better for them if you told', Gaby followed suit. While the boys in the group, Donald, Graham and Tony began by defending the rabbi, by the end of the discussion, only Donald seemed unshaken in his position.

A student whose views were absolutely unflinching and fundamentally opposed to informing on the rabbi, was the Italian student Marco. While in discussion his friends Michael and Greg, as well as Louise — the only girl in the group —posed the question of loyalty towards his own family, Marco remained adamant that the central issue was about 'a person's life':

> 'If the Rabbi is found out well there you are. You can't turn him away just like that. It would be inhuman, even if you are endangering other people's lives.'

Amongst those who acknowledged from their first response that they would probably give the rabbi up, a couple expressed guilt, but most were concerned with presenting their reasons. The most common was that of protecting one's family. An additional justification for Andrew, however, was that the rabbi was 'old and wrinckled'. Andrew, who had lived in South Africa for seven years, was sensitive to racist connotations on black/white issues and often appeared to attempt a 'cover up' of his own feelings when he sensed these might not be appropriate. For instance he would sometimes make an obviously 'moralist' statement. At other times he would be slightly 'jokey', so if necessary he could perhaps disengage himself from responsibility by the claim 'I was only joking'. In his written response to the rabbi issue, he considered the likelihood of torture and made a distinction between helping the Schneiders ('my friends') and the rabbi:

> 'I wouldn't endanger myself just for a stranger because I don't even know what he is like.'

When challenged in discussion to consider the consequences for the rabbi, he descended to giggling:

> SIMON: You actually have got a choice in the matter, in keeping the secret or not.
>
> ANDREW: Yeah but..the Rabbi was old and um.. I wouldn't endanger my life for just an old person like him! (giggling).... he's a Rabbi! 'Cause I don't like him! (giggle) 'Cause he's a Jew! (giggle)

Of the nine students saying they would inform, only two were girls and one of these — Tanya — changed her position in discussion, probably as a result of the argument being put in strongly moral terms by her friend Angela. Both Erica and Tanya posed a primary loyalty to family, but nevertheless spoke of guilt. All the seven boys apart from Andrew had scored within the medium high to high range on the Racist Perceptions Survey. While John (the highest scorer on the first survey) seemed to face a problem of guilt and whether he had 'the guts' to tell the rabbi to his face to leave, in his written response Ian appeared more concerned about remaining anonymous:

> '...I would inform the government but on the quiet so nobody knows it was me. But I would still treat them as a friend but in a disguished manner. The pressure they are under at the moment I think death would relief them of all the pressure... '

Thus he appeared to absolve himself from guilt by suggesting that death would provide relief from suffering for presumably the Schneiders as well as the rabbi. In his group discussion Ian went beyond articulating this rationalisation which was challenged, in particular by Angela. He went on to reveal that he made a fundamental distinction between 'German' and 'Jew':

> IAN: ...I think it's better to die because he is under great pressure isn't he?
>
> ANGELA: Who?
>
> IAN: Er.. the Snider whatever his name is Herr-
>
> ANGELA: No I am talking about the narrator. I think he should let the rabbi stay.

JOHN: Even though I would have said, I don't think I would have been able to say it straight out because you have to build up a lot of guts to say in front of a man to go somewhere else.

IAN: But isn't the narrator a German, not a Jew?

ANGELA: But the whole idea of the argument is not---

IAN: Yeah but why should he be saving a Jew when he's a German?

ANGELA: Because he's good friends with Friedrich.

TANYA: Yeah.

NEIL: Yeah, he wouldn't want to grass Friedrich up because they have been friends since..(background interruption) What? Yeah-

ANGELA: So what do you think... why do you say about the Germans and the Jews?

IAN: Well I don't know um er..

ANGELA: So Ian hasn't got a comment to back up his-

IAN: Yes I have right..um I think then (laughter in background)

ANGELA: Come on then.

IAN: I think that he should be defending himself. He shouldn't get himself killed for something for another Jew. Why didn't the Jew save the Jew?

ANGELA: That's what they are trying to do. He didn't find out about it until then. They are trying to save him, the Jewish family are. I don't think you can back that up really Ian. What are your feelings about that? Tanya can't talk!

TANYA: Well I think he should let the rabbi stay.

It was not surprising that Ian suggested in his journal that 'it would of been better if you let Angela compete against somebody who will overpower her'. He was indeed forced to the point where he expressed his basic construct of a fundamental difference between Germans and Jews. As already indicated by some of Ian's responses during *Buddy*, he held deeply embedded notions of difference and what constitutes normality.

Language and power

The use of the words 'German' and 'Jew' as referring to contrasting categories of people was questioned on one occasion by the teacher, but nevertheless this use remained fairly widespread amongst the students. Far more time would have been required to develop an awareness of the use of language in embodying and perpetuating notions of difference and to raise questions about the links between language, status and power. During the reading of *Friedrich*, Alan Parsons undertook a brief activity in which the students listed all the 'nicknames' they knew relating to groups of people. They were also asked to write the contexts in which they had either heard these words used, or possibly used them themselves. The combined lists consisted of 121 different names, almost all of them clearly derogatory.

This activity was followed by a class discussion in which the teacher attempted to lead the students towards viewing name-calling as a process of dehumanisation and reduction of others. However it was questionable whether the didactic question-and-answer form of the lesson encouraged the students to begin their own meaningful exploration of the issues — especially in relation to their own feelings and language use. Even students like Angela and Neil at times used the term 'the Jew' to refer to the rabbi — unconscious perhaps of its depersonalising effect. The extract above gives an example of Ian's extremely casual and dismissive approach to naming certain people: 'Er.. the Snider whatever his name is Herr-'. Conscious or unconscious, the effect is to belittle the owner of the name. My feeling with Ian was that the effect was frequently calculated.

Public and private spaces for response

Ian was not the only student who said he would have given the rabbi away anonymously. Terry was likewise concerned to distance himself from any danger. He quite openly stated his only ethic as that of self-preservation:

> '...I would tell the nazis but not myself. I would send them a letter just incase they arrested me thinking I've known all along. The reason I would tell is because I wouldn't be so stupid as to risk my neck for the sake of a stranger and a jew that I don't even know the name of.'

As an afterthought he mentioned that if he got to know the rabbi and liked him, he 'might have second thoughts'. Nevertheless in his discussion group Terry maintained a straightforward 'chuck him out' position. The more other students asked him to consider the consequences, the more he appeared to thrive on establishing his 'hard man' image:

PETER: How would they live on the streets then Terry?

TERRY: Well no that's it! That's his problem!

ALISON: But the Germans are coming round..

PAUL: Don't you feel any sympathy for him if he had to go to concentration camp and all that?

TERRY: He's a stranger. I don't know him.

ALISON: Yeah but it doesn't matter! It doesn't matter if he is a stranger!

PAUL: I bet his face would look really sad.

ALISON: So what if he is a Jew?

TERRY (chanting): Chuck him out!

While Terry's response appeared to contain a marked element of playing to the audience, in his journal he appeared to allow himself the occasional comment reflecting more sensitive emotions — although it is of course possible that he was simply writing what he thought would be appropriate. For instance at the end of the novel, he wrote about Friedrich 'I thought it was sad that he died at such a young age and I thought Herr Resch should of felt really guilty.' Terry's responses tended to remain at a fairly crude, limited level and he didn't appear at all disconcerted about contradictions. For instance in relation to the pogrom (when the narrator himself became involved in smashing up the Jewish home for apprentices) he wrote:

'It was funny when he got his hammer and started being destructive with it but it was pretty sad about what happened in the Snieders house and Friedrick and his mum and dad. '

Terry seemed unable to make any link between what he found 'funny' and what he found 'sad'. In contrast, at least six other boys admitted in their journals to identifying in some way with the narrator and the pleasure of taking part in the violence, but seemed to have some self-awareness of the implications. Like the narrator on returning to see the destruction of Friedrich's home, it seems that they were forced to look, albeit briefly, at themselves. Paul recorded his response to the pogrom with considerable honesty:

'Unbelievable. This shook my bones. I nearly found myself chanting with the book. Towards the end, when Hans was smashing everything up, I to found pleasure of seeing and smashing glass. This was because there was no-one in the world to stop (you) him. It was even more disturbing reading that Frau Schneider had been killed. I can't put into words the sadness I felt because it took me by surprise so much.'

Paul's slip into the pronoun 'you', subsequently corrected to 'him', reinforces all he was saying and reveals that even as he was writing, his sense of identification with the narrator was intense. A passage such as this indicates the tremendous value of the reading journal and the relatively more private space it provided for personal exploration and reflection. At the end of the first term Tanya wrote in hers: 'These journals have been a god-send (I've managed to stay sain by writing in these).' Even for a student with what appeared a very limited range of responses like Terry, it was possible to see him at least use the term 'sad' within the privacy of his journal, while in public discussion he consistently sought to maintain the 'macho' stance of indifference.

Throughout the year I was conscious of the difficulty in trying to offer the students space to articulate and explore their own responses honestly while at the same time presenting challenges to racist thinking in ways that would not provoke either simply defensive reactions or result in the students just giving what they thought was required i.e. a 'correct' response. The issue is of central importance and is one which will be revisited in chapters that follow.

Moral dilemmas: 'Time for Judgement'

In a number of the response sheets the students were left to determine their own focus in making their jottings around the text. However with both the extract taken from the chapter 'The Rabbi' and in a subsequent sheet entitled 'Time for Judgement', the students' attention was sharply focused on particular moral issues. In both they were required to make decisions and in the latter indeed to judge the narrator's parents. As with responses concerning the rabbi, I was as interested in the basis on which judgements were formed as the decision itself. I had no wish to encourage the students to become simplistically judgemental.

The 'Time for Judgement' session took place in the final week of term after the students had completed reading *Friedrich,* with unfortunately only twenty-one of the thirty students present. They were taken into the drama room for a double period and initially asked to re-enact the final scene 'In The Shelter'. In this penultimate chapter, the narrator's family have left Friedrich hiding in their flat while they respond to an air-raid warning to go to the communal shelter. Although the narrator's mother had wanted to take Friedrich with them, his father had said it would be impossible as Herr Resch, their landlord and official warden, would have him imprisoned. As the bombing gets worse there is a sudden pounding on the door and a terrified Friedrich begs to be let in. Despite pleas from many in the shelter not to turn the boy away, Resch refuses and threatens to report anyone who persists in contradicting him. The final chapter records how, when the raid is over, Friedrich is found dead on the steps outside the house.

After first re-enacting the text as it stood, the students were asked to replay the scene, but this time Alan Parsons suggested that they could change events if they wished, in any way they felt feasible. This led to a version in which the narrator's father (played by John) physically confronted Herr Resch (played by Donald). The father backed down, however, when Resch pulled out a gun and Friedrich remained excluded from the shelter. This re-enactment was followed by the narrator's mother (Alison) and his father (John) each being hotseated by the class and the teacher. Questions revolved around why the father had joined the Nazi Party, whether both parents felt they had done enough for Friedrich and his family, whether they blamed themselves at all, and what they thought of Herr Resch.

The hotseating was followed by a 'sociogramming' exercise in which John was asked to stand on a chair in a central position, representing the narrator's father, while the other students were asked to stand near or far away from him to demonstrate the degree of sympathy each personally felt for him. The exercise was then repeated with Alison representing the narrator's mother. On both occasions Donald remained the furthest away, indicating uncompromising criticism. While the majority of students started close in to the narrator's father (no doubt indicating a degree of peer group conformity as well as sympathy), there was some shifting outwards to a moderately critical position. However with the narrator's mother in the centre, there was a perceptible move inwards.

Finally the students were given the 'Time for Judgement' sheets. These consisted of a couple of questions about individual ability to resist group pressure and the issue of putting the comfort and safety of one's own family first before responding to the persecution of others. The students were asked to imagine the narrator's parents were on trial and charged with breaking two moral laws from Leviticus:

'Thou shalt not stand idly by the blood of thy neighbour.'

'Thou shalt love thy neighbour as thyself.'

Everyone was asked first to consider a personal verdict in relation to both parents and to state on what they based their opinion, before deciding in self-selected groups on a group verdict and giving the reasoning behind that as well.

The boys' responses

With the exception of Donald and partially of Marco (who found the mother guilty of not doing enough for Friedrich) all the boys found both the narrator's father and mother not guilty. They generally felt that the two of them were not personally against Friedrich and had done everything they could. To have done more would have been to risk their own lives and this was not considered a reasonable option. In other words, they saw pragmatic self-preservation as an acceptable defence. Donald, who in the sociogram had physically distanced himself the furthest from both the narrator's parents, remained a lone dissenter. Commenting on his group's verdict of 'Not Guilty' he wrote:

'I didn't want this. they forced me. I disagreed and wanted both guilty they were both getting income and protection from the nazi party.'

It is worth noting that both Donald and Marco involved a parent when subsequently making their taped responses to the Holocaust at home, which in both cases revealed that they had Jewish relations. It also worth recalling that both Donald and Marco firmly took the position of defending the rabbi when others in their group were wavering.

The girls' responses

The responses of the girls provided a sharp contrast to that of the boys, with the majority tending to find both parents guilty. However many of them appeared to have experienced more conflict or uncertainty than the boys in making their personal decisions, judging from the amount of crossing out of original responses. A few girls also made a distinction between the two laws of Leviticus, and expressed different verdicts accordingly. For instance, Erica and Caroline found the parents guilty on the charge of standing 'idly by the blood of thy neighbour' but not guilty with regard to 'Thou shalt love thy neighbour as thyself'. Caroline reasoned that they had tried to protect Friedrich but 'They couldn't really do anything about it because they were pressured by Herr Resch.'

Two other girls proposing verdicts of 'not guilty' were Louise and Michelle. Although Louise found the father 'slightly guilty because he joined the party but was still a friend to the Schneiders', she felt the mother should not be blamed. Michelle's 'not guilty' response however, seemed to be based on the father's personal right to join the Nazi party if he wished and the financial pressure for him to do so. Interestingly, Louise and Michelle were the only girls in a mixed group. Their verdicts may possibly have been different had they been in a girls' only group.

Most of the girls were clustered in two discussion groups which appeared to combine around Angela. The conversation recorded on a nearby tape recorder reveals that she was influential at an early stage of the discussion by raising the question of the French Resistance and the possibility of resistance. She also made the point that had Friedrich been their own child, the narrator's parents would not have left him behind in the house. A further point raised by Gaby was that the threat of having their house taken away from them was over-rated as 'it might have been bombed down by the time the raid had finished'.

My general impression of the responses to the sheet was that most of the students could find strong justification for pragmatic compromise, in terms of preserving personal safety, but that amongst the girls this line of argument was more actively countered by a sense of conscience. The girls also appeared more inclined to explore affective dimensions of the situation in greater depth — hence focusing on protection of a child and considering how a family could actually leave a child behind during a bombing raid.

Perceptions of relevance

Final responses to Friedrich were made in reading journals as well as on tape — either individually or in pairs, over the Christmas holidays. As a framework for making their tapes, students were given a couple of sheets entitled 'The Holocaust' containing some illustrations, quotations from Cardinal Hume and the Archbishop of Canterbury on the Christian involvement and responsibility, as well as Pastor Niemoeller's poem 'First They Came For

The Jews' (Bayfield 1981). Students were asked to imagine they were making a radio programme on 'What a young person today thinks about the Holocaust'. It was suggested they might include responses to some questions and items on the sheet, and that they might also wish to interview people. While the tapes from a few students suggested they had been involved in little more than an exercise, there were others which suggested real involvement. Donald and Marco (the only boys who had laid some blame on the narrator's parents) each interviewed a parent, who spoke about Jewish relatives within the family. Marco's step-aunt and uncle had actually escaped from Auschwitz. It seems likely that this family connection may well have affected these students' responses to the novel. Parental interest was most likely also a factor for Michael whose Polish grandfather came to England at the time of the war, apparently as part of the Polish Resistance. In his tape Michael not only spoke of feeling sad, upset and angry but also of his father visiting Auschwitz after the war and of 'the terrible feeling to stand there'.

It was not only students who had some form of family basis for personal identification with events of the Holocaust however, who acknowledged that it had some personal meaning for them. Asked about this wider context rather than more specifically the novel itself, there again seemed to be a rather interesting gender difference. Whereas three-quarters of the boys acknowledged on their tapes that the Holocaust was not totally distant and had some meaning for them, only a third of the girls said they felt it meant something to them today. Yet many girls had offered sensitive commentaries while reading *Friedrich*. This is not an area I investigated but it raises the question of whether some girls saw the wider subject of 'The Holocaust' as part of a political and male-dominated domain to which they felt they had little connection.

In addition the stimulus sheet which formed the basis of their taped responses contained quotations only from men (The Archbishop of Canterbury, Cardinal Hume and Pastor Niemoeller). The illustrations also reflected a slight male bias although the most striking was probably that of a young girl wearing a star of David. In their initial responses to the cover of the book the majority of girls had identified it unenthusiastically as a 'boy's book' or about war (e.g. Julia: 'Oh no! a war story — how boring.'). Although this initial reaction appeared to be somewhat dispelled, judging by the quality of involvement in responses from those same girls in their journals, nevertheless it appeared from final journal comments to have been enjoyed by a notably greater proportion of boys than girls. It was, however, difficult to know to what extent Angela's response, for instance, was largely a reaction against the fact that all the books they had previously been asked to read in St Mary's had featured male central characters:

'Interesting and informative but I still didn't enjoy the book, it was too repetitive and I don't think it gave enough information about the persecution of the jews. It was to much based on a boys life from the view of another...I think we should have a book based on a girls life or feeling or opinions about society... I have enjoyed this term... The english lessons we have had have been the most interesting since I came to this school.'

The apparent contradictions (enjoying the lessons but not the book) possibly derive from Angela's desire to make a strong statement about gender bias in the books they had read. However a number of other students, male and female, also commented on the novel being repetitive and at times 'a list of events' (e.g. Jacky, Peter). Alison's final journal comment was that

'...the subject, that is the Jews, was very intresting to read about, but the book was simple and repeated itself many times. I would like to find out more information about the Jews...'

Perhaps these comments indicate a response to Richter's spare, emotionally contained style — the simplicity of which is deceptive. Even with the boys, amongst whom the book was largely popular with only one exception, a number had referred to it being repetitive at times. Such comments suggest a tendency to reduce the novel to a cognitive message. Given time, it would have been useful to encourage students to explore Richter's style and help counter the notion that the author was involved in a 'simple' exercise of conveying the knowledge of 'facts'.

Evidence for the importance of students having different spaces and contexts in which to develop responses is provided by the dialogues in which both Angela and Alison engaged when making their tapes, each with a close friend. These took place after their end-of-term reviews on Friedrich where the context had tended to encourage them to formulate and finalise their individual judgements on the book. Angela chose to make her tape with Tanya, who had also commented in her review that the novel was, with the exception of some chapters, repetitive and boring. The most striking feature of their taped conversation, however, was the degree to which they related issues of exclusion, identity and injustice to their own lives while referring into the text, as well as drawing on other experiences from the term such as a drama session and *Buddy*. It seems probable that privacy was an important factor in enabling the discussion to move into sensitive areas of personal identity. Each described to the other an incident when she had felt 'put down'. Angela's was an occasion when someone had identified her as Irish and therefore 'thick':

ANGELA: I think that everybody should be proud of what they are.. I don't think it's.. I don't think the idea of living in a society with different races and cultures is that you become a different race or a different culture yourself (TANYA: Yeah) you just stay an individual.. and think that you should.. you should stick up for other people.. as an individual and as a group (TANYA: Yeah, yeah) and um.. like if you were Jewish.. (TANYA: Mmm) actually I don't know what I would do if you were Jewish if.. if it was back then..

TANYA: Yeah, yeah it's quite hard isn't it?

ANGELA: It's quite hard to think.. Yeah.. you are put under a lot of pressure.. and sometimes you can't tell your parents what's going on. (TANYA: Yeah) You feel really distant to them. Something happens to you and it.. you think it's their fault because.. like if my parents were Chinese and I was born in this country and people started taking the mick out of me I would think it was their fault.

TANYA: Oh yes that's what we've done in that other drama lesson isn't it with Mr. Parsons.. with those um.. those two kids.. I can't remember the names.. what was it? Jesuit that's it.

ANGELA: Oh the Scavvies.

TANYA: Mm.. yeah.

ANGELA: Yeah they were called nicknames, the Scavs or something.. (pause) I wouldn't know what to do! I wouldn't.. if we were split up! It has never happened to me that seriously. I think that was the only time (TANYA: Mmm) and I felt really hurt then... [referring to the incident when she had been called 'thick'] That's why I try not to bring up.. I don't know why I'm.. I'm proud that I'm Irish but I try not bring up the fact that I am (TANYA: Mmm) unless somebody says something about them that offends.. me and my.. my country I suppose.

TANYA: Yeah.. yeah but I.. I don't know.. I probably wouldn't stick up for anything English.. it it's difficult cause you're in an English country.. cause you are not in Ireland any more either (ANGELA: No) so.. um.. cause you're in England and everybody else is in England.. cause if I went over to Ireland I probably would stick up for the English.

ANGELA (sounding a little surprised): Stick up for the English?

TANYA: Yeah.

ANGELA: The Irish.. well I don't think they'd say anything anyway.

TANYA: No no I doubt if they would.

ANGELA: They're not like that.

The transcript suggests an active involvement with *Friedrich*. Angela, having made a statement on the right of individuals to maintain different cultural identities, suddenly challenged herself to consider her response had she and Tanya found themselves in the context of the novel with Tanya being Jewish. There were no easy answers and the discussion moved on to the pressures to conform and the high price of non-conformity. Angela indicated her own strategy of not calling attention to being Irish — essentially a strategy of assimilation — unless she felt her personal or cultural pride were at stake. She would no doubt have found it hard to define the criteria for this. As mentioned previously, on one occasion she was part of a small group of students who unwittingly recorded themselves engaging in a racist joking session during their drama session on the theme of intolerance. Initiated by Ian — very likely to subvert the theme of the lesson — Angela actually contributed an anti-Irish piece on 'talking backwards'.

As in group situations, Angela was the dominant contributor, tending to direct the discussion with Tanya, often by asking probing questions about how Tanya would have responded. For instance, she wanted to know how Tanya would have felt if she had been a child in Friedrich's class when he was excluded:

ANGELA: If you were in that class what would you have done?

TANYA: What would I have done? Um.. (said forcefully as if stuck) There's not a lot I.. I don't know! There's not a lot you could do is there? Cause you've no authority isn't it? The teacher and that..

ANGELA: What if you were.. if you were that Jewish child and nobody said anything to you.. (TANYA: Mmm..) Supposing, I know, the teacher didn't insult him, but supposing the teacher subtly insulted his culture or whatever, and you were the Jewish child and nobody stuck up for you, how would you feel?

TANYA: Really hurt.. really hurt that nobody stuck up for me.

ANGELA: And yet you've just said that you wouldn't have stuck up for him.. so aren't you really criticising.. um contradicting yourself?

TANYA: Yeah! (embarrassed laugh)

ANGELA: So why do you think that is? Do you think it's.. Do you think it.. I I think.. Well do you think that it would be.. um.. it's not.. it's harder to stick up for someone than it is to want someone to stick up for you?

TANYA: Yeah.. yeah.

This extract not only indicates Angela's powerful ability to probe, but I have quoted it without abbreviation to show how she herself was attempting to sort out some of her own thoughts in the process and to make sense of the moral/ pragmatic contradictions she no doubt experienced herself. Although Angela took the lead throughout, Tanya was an active listener.

It could be argued that *Friedrich* might be more productively read with students older than thirteen. Certainly it presented a considerably greater challenge than *Buddy*. Caroline, for instance, raised the question of age:

> 'I thought that the book would have been better and I would understand it more if I had read it in a few years time.. It would mean more to me. The work that was set to do with Friedrich was good and I think I understood it better and could get into it when there was drama or t.v. programmes as a follow up... If a girl was in the same situation as Friedrich I wonder if her views would have been the same.'

This gender question was yet another indication of the desire amongst the girls for a reflection of female experience in their class literature. On the other hand, the male hero had not proved a total deterrent to Hannah whose initial response had been 'Oh no, another male 'heroic story':

> 'This book was more moving than Buddy was... I was proved wrong as at first I thought it was going to be very boring.'

A number of male students recorded it as having made quite a significant impact on them, for example:

> 'I think Friedrich is one of the best books I have ever read... Before I read the book I found it hard to grasp the idea that all the terror had actually happened but now I can.' (Philip)

> 'I was astonished that this story was true. When I was younger I had no idea what the Nazis did to the Jews but now my dreams are shattered as I read the true story of the Holocaust.' (Paul)

> 'My thoughts and views of the book... have completely changed... it spotlights to me quite a few facts. Mainly that the Jews who died during the time of the Nazi dictatorship were real people and not only facts and figures. The book kept me interested and I did something I dont normally do with English class readers which is read on.' (Carl)

Carl has not only highlighted here the power of literature in bringing home to him that the 'the Jews who died... were real people and not only facts and figures' from history but in addition he ended with one extremely pertinent question embedded in another:

> 'There is only one question which remains in my mind which is, what the subject of the persecution of the Jews has to do with us and why in History matters like this are only skipped over without touching the heart of the matter.'

Unless teaching about racism can indeed touch 'the heart of the matter' for students, the question 'What has it to do with us?' is likely to persist.

Chapter Five

The challenge of a Black American perspective — responses to Roll of Thunder, Hear My Cry

Outline of *Roll of Thunder, Hear My Cry* and related activities

Set during the depression of the 1930s, Mildred Taylor's novel is a powerful evocation of the American south, seen through the eyes of a young black girl, nine-year old Cassie Logan. The only black land-owning family in the area, the Logans are determined to resist pressure from the big white land-owner Harlan Granger to sell their land and become reduced to share-cropping. While Cassie and her three brothers — Stacey, Christopher-John and Little Man — learn the harsh realities of living under white power, they also learn from their family about principles of fundamental human dignity and resistance to injustice. When a neighbouring black family suffers death and permanent injury through a racist attack in which the Wallaces — the white family running the local store — are implicated, Cassie's parents organise a boycott of the Wallaces' shop. They do so with full knowledge of the serious possible consequences for themselves.

The Logans extend across three generations, with Big Ma (Cassie's grandmother), Papa and Mama each conveying to the children, through memories and stories, a sense of their history — a history which the author found denied and distorted in her own schooling. Two characters outside the Logan family, however, seemed to me to be central to the students' under-standing of the novel. The first, T.J., son of a poor black share-cropping family, is the untrustworthy friend of Cassie's older brother Stacey. His desire to be 'someone' leads to a tragic conclusion. Believing he is being offered the superior friendship of two white men (R.W. and Melvin Simms), T.J. becomes involved in a burglary which ends in the Simms' brothers murdering a white shopkeeper and laying the blame on the boy T.J.

The second character only appears occasionally but provides a key counterpoise to T.J. in his relationship with Stacey. He is the white boy Jeremy, younger brother of the Simms, who persists in genuinely wanting to be friends with the Logan children despite being treated with sustained wariness and suspicion. He is furthermore undeterred by being beaten by his father for associating with a black family. I was particularly interested to see how the students would interpret Jeremy's rejection by the Logan children. To what extent would they be able to transcend their own frames of reference and expectations concerning friendship to understand the constraints of the power divide depicted in the novel?

As with *Friedrich*, it was necessary to give the students some idea of the historical and social context out of which the novel arose. This was done through the English Centre's excellent background book (1984) and The English Programme (1988) interview with Mildred Taylor, filmed at her family's home in Mississippi. A further means of addressing the students' unfamiliarity with experiences of the novel and racism was to invite the writer Millie Murray for a workshop, the major part of which was a hotseating session where she took on consecutively the roles of the three generations of female characters (Chapter Seven).

Apart from their journal writing, students engaged in a number of oral and written assignments, including responding to specific passages and 'thought-tracking' characters at particular points i.e. writing their inner thoughts. They were introduced to some black American poetry and their drama lessons focused on exploring issues of oppression. These included their own experiences of injustice; adult-child as well as sibling relationships linked to power; and questions of status and power in an inter-school conflict.

Initial responses from the girls on receiving the book were particularly positive (e.g. 'great, a girl heroine!' — Tanya). While two-thirds of the boys expressed either positive expectations or were non-committal, a third predicted the book would be boring. John, for instance, identified it as 'a girl's book' and Ian said it did not 'look over brilliant... it is just like discrimination between whites and blacks'. Carl too thought 'it will be rather boring and just about black minorities who are being racially harassed... perhaps I may be wrong about the book like I was about the last one.' The word 'just' suggests both these boys were ready to predict a didactic message which could easily be dismissed as 'boring'. Carl was however prepared to admit his prediction could be wrong, and indeed that proved to be the case for him as with most of the others.

Students' perceptions of the Logans' wariness towards Jeremy

The first passage for specific focus came from Chapter Three, where the white bus driver, with a bus-load of white children shouting abuse, deliberately veers towards the group of black children forcing them into a mud-filled gully. Immediately afterwards Jeremy approaches them with a friendly smile, but gets no response. Only after he leaves them to walk up to the white school, does Cassie realise that Jeremy never travels on the white bus, however bad the weather. The students were asked first to write their thoughts and feelings alongside the passage and then to answer the following questions:

> Where do you feel you are when reading this passage? Are you inside the story with particular characters, or viewing the events as an outside onlooker? Or does your position perhaps change? If so, how?

Apart from my own interest in learning about the kind of identifications the students were making with the characters, the intention of the task was for the students themselves to become more aware of their perspectives and to reflect on how these were possibly being formed. Had there been time this kind of activity could have been very usefully developed to help students reflect more on how texts are constructed by both writer and reader.

At least half the students commented on Jeremy in their responses to the passage, a quarter indicating they felt the Logans should have been friendlier towards him, a sentiment expressed by other students as well elsewhere. For instance, Jacky wrote in her response:

> 'As the white kids have hurt Stacy he can't really communicate with any other white kids as it hurts and reminds him of what has happened. I think this is a horrible judgement to make, just cause one white kid acts one way that doesn't mean to say all white kids act that way. Cassie suddenly realises they have done wrong and should not be horrible to Jeremy.'

Interestingly, in her analysis of where she felt she was placed when reading, Jacky identified herself as having begun the book as 'an outsider, looking in on their 'world' but as the book progresses I was in Cassy's position'. Her condemnation of the Logan children's response to Jeremy revealed however her own white perspective predominating at this point. Her statement 'just cause one white kid acts one way that doesn't mean to say all white kids act that way' has turned the circumstances of the text around since it is all the white children except Jeremy who 'act that way'. Rather than being able to consider what Stacey's 'hurt' really felt like — including the full extent of its cause — her response appeared to derive rather from a concern not to be considered racist because of the behaviour of another white person. This also indicates a conception of racism limited to personal behaviour, attitude and relationships — a conception which was common throughout the class as well as within the teacher's thinking. Yet it would be difficult to understand the Logans' deep wariness of Jeremy without some understanding of how, despite his admirable personal qualities, Jeremy was nevertheless part of a society structured in terms of power and inequality.

Within the novel, Stacey experiences a real conflict in relation to Jeremy. Had Jeremy been black, he and Stacey would no doubt have been close friends. Instead Stacey is left with T.J. who is not merely untrustworthy but maliciously unscrupulous. Mildred Taylor brings the issue of friendship in a divided and unequal society to a fine focus when Jeremy brings a home-made flute for Stacey and a bag of nuts for the Logan family at Christmas. Not only is he defying convention and risking punishment from his own family, but he is also clearly nervous about his reception at the Logans. The children's Uncle Hammer, who has returned on a visit from the North, is openly hostile. After Jeremy has left, Stacey questions his father about the possibility of allowing the friendship to develop. Papa firmly points out, however, that friendship across the colour line is usually not on an equal basis. While Jeremy will grow up to be a man, Stacey will quite probably remain a 'boy' to him:

> Maybe one day whites and blacks can be real friends, but right now the country ain't built that way. Now you could be right 'bout Jeremy making a much finer friend than T.J. ever will be. The trouble is, down here in Mississippi, it costs too much to find out. (p.119)

That night Cassie sees Stacey silently fingering the flute Jeremy had brought him, before carefully placing it in a box of treasured things, from which she never sees him take it out again.

After reading this passage, the students were asked to write responses in their reading journals. While a number of students did not comment on what they personally thought of Papa's advice to Stacey, of those who did the majority felt the friendship should be allowed to develop. One can only speculate on how much this was due to a sense of identity with Jeremy on the basis of colour. Neil, for instance, indicated a real involvement with Jeremy:

> 'I'm very proud of Jeremy for bringing the nuts and the flute for Stacey. I was half expecting Uncle Hammers reaction to what Stacey told him about Jeremy. However, I don't think Jeremy would be like that in later years.'

Neil's use of the word 'proud' suggests a strong identification with Jeremy, whose individual actions probably represented as positive a rejection as possible of the 'race' divide for a white child in those circumstances. A number of other students asserted that Jeremy would be different from what Papa predicted. Not only did they conceptualise racism at a purely personal level (i.e. as long as Jeremy was not 'racist', friendship should not be a problem), but they appeared to have considerable faith in Jeremy as an individual. Papa was seen as being 'a bit harsh' (Andrew), 'quite narrow minded' (Angela) and generally judging Jeremy incorrectly: 'I feel sorry for Jeremy and I think Papa judges him completely wrong' (Donald).

Caroline's response gave evidence of real concern about the problem. While acknowledging that Papa 'does have a reason', she too felt 'it sounds as if he is being racist'. Perceiving Jeremy as an individual caught between two communities — 'he just can't win' — she not only affirmed Jeremy's potential to turn out differently from his father, but proposed that the only way out of the impasse of 'race' conflict is for individuals to break rank:

> 'If I was Stacy I would go around with Jeremy because I know that Jeremy is kind and would never turn on me. It isn't Jeremy's fault he was born white, he would much rather be black. He doesn't really fit in with either colour but he disagrees with white folk so he turns to the blacks. No body will give him a chance. Papa says to Stacy that one day whites and blacks could be real friends. That will never be until someone starts being friendly to someone else of a different colour they could see that not everyone is out to get one another and then nobody would care whether people were black or white.'

While there can be no doubt about the sincerity of Caroline's desire for a moral revolution of individuals, it is also clear that her conception of racism does not extend beyond one of inter-personal hostility.

A small number of students commenting on Papa's advice to Stacey, did however express support for Papa's viewpoint. Of the five students, four seemed to do so on the basis that the relationship with Jeremy could cause Stacey hurt or trouble later. Indeed Paul suggested that Papa may have been talking from personal experience.

Terry's support for Papa seemed, however, to have a different basis, although this was not immediately obvious from his journal response. It was in a taped discussion which turned to the Jeremy/Stacey relationship that his actual racist frame of reference was sharply revealed:

PAUL: Jeremy's got guts to miss the bus.

TERRY: He should hang around with his own kind.

Subsequent comments by Terry on the Logans revealed a distinct lack of sympathy for them. Thus while for the other students who supported Papa's advice, the division between Jeremy and Stacey nevertheless appeared to be a matter for regret, for Terry the issue seemed simply to be that each should keep to 'his own kind' — in other words, that each should accept the philosophy of apartheid.

The teacher's response to a black perspective

A brief discussion directed by the teacher followed the journal writing session on the passage about Papa's advice. Although his line of questioning was very probably influenced by what he perceived as my particular interest in student perceptions of the power dimension, the questions he formulated seemed to suggest that he himself did not altogether accept Papa's position:

> A.P.: ...Were you shocked by Papa's line?... Were you shocked by that view? (Pause) John?
>
> JOHN: Um there was truth in it somewhere.. but um I think it was a bit harsh to tell a boy.. sort of when he's got friends... he's saying that his friends are all.. could possibly betray him later on in life... I don't think I'd say that sort of thing.
>
> A.P.: You think Papa was being harsh?
>
> JOHN: Yeah. (Bell)
>
> A.P.: Graham?
>
> GRAHAM: I think that's more the sort of thing that Uncle Hammer would have said.. towards whites. I didn't realise that um Papa didn't like whites so much.
>
> A.P.: So you think Papa.. Papa was showing um a slightly less liberal attitude than you would have thought he might earlier on?
>
> GRAHAM: Mm.
>
> PAUL: Maybe Papa had already experienced.. he had a white friend when he was a boy and his friend had turned against him.
>
> A.P.: Possibly.. that would have accounted for it. Right I'm going to leave it there.

While the teacher was constrained by this taking place at the end of the lesson when there was no time to explore adequately the students' responses, his questions appeared nevertheless to be phrased in a way likely to reinforce a closed view of Papa. Rather than asking an open-ended 'What were your responses to Papa's advice?' he asked 'Were you shocked by Papa's line?' When John replied that he felt Papa was being 'a bit harsh', instead of enquiring how this perception could be reconciled with Papa's desire to protect Stacey from future hurt, the teacher simply asked John to confirm 'You think Papa was being harsh?' Furthermore when Graham added the comment 'I didn't realise that um Papa didn't like whites so much', Alan Parsons did not suggest that they perhaps needed to look at that idea further in another lesson — i.e. examine whether it really was a matter simply of Papa not 'liking whites'. Instead he raised the possibility of Papa being 'less liberal' than previously supposed. Although Paul's suggestion that Papa may have actually had personal experience of rejection by a former white friend was acknowledged, the lesson had to end.

The teacher's line of questioning here (which was not isolated and had indeed been presaged by his questions on the black boy Dennis in *Buddy*) seemed to me indicative that it was not only the students who had difficulty in being able to imagine and identify with the psychological reality of oppression. While there was a tendency amongst some students to interpret the wariness of black characters towards sympathetic white people as evidence of their fundamentally 'not liking' whites, Alan Parsons appeared to question the Logans' response in terms of fundamental notions of being 'liberal' and presumably 'balanced'.

In the next lesson, a similar issue arose in discussion about the reaction of Papa and Uncle Hammer to the supportive white lawyer Mr Jamison. Hammer appears particularly wary of the lawyer who offers his own money to back the credit required by the black sharecroppers in order to continue boycotting the local white store and buy their goods further afield in Vicksburg. Mr Jamison explains that he does not want to see the Logans lose their land, which would certainly happen if they stood credit for the share-cropping families. The teacher's questions focused mainly on understanding the lawyer's perspective:

> A.P.: He's actually going to offer his own money as surety for the credit that the black families are going to need to do their shopping in Vicksburg as opposed to the Wallaces. What's his motivation for doing that?...
>
> PHILIP: He doesn't like whites any more than they do.
>
> A.P.: No that's not the point. 'He doesn't like whites any more than they do'. (repeated in dismissive tone)
>
> MARION: He doesn't like what they are doing to the black families.
>
> A.P.: Yes! He feels a sense of injustice.. just as much. Would you say Uncle Hammer's response to him was a bit harsh.. He seems very suspicious. Philip?
>
> PHILIP: Um.. it is a bit yeah.
>
> A.P.: And how does Mr Jamison answer that suspicion?

Here Alan Parsons elicited a distinction between Mr Jamison not disliking white people per se but disliking what they were doing to black people — the distinction between hating injustice, but not the perpetrators in themselves. It was interesting that he immediately questioned Philip's simple notion of Mr Jamison 'not liking whites' whereas he did not raise this query in relation to similar ideas about Papa. While in the previous lesson he had not queried John's interpretation of Papa as being 'a bit harsh' about Jeremy, here he himself suggested to the students — through the use of closed questions — that Uncle Hammer's response to Mr Jamison was 'a bit harsh' and 'suspicious'. It appeared that Alan Parsons — with his desire for a 'balanced' response — found it easier to identify with the white lawyer (whom he perceived as feeling 'a sense of injustice.. just as much' as the black recipients) than with either Papa or Uncle Hammer whose actual experience of oppression over many years had led them to be extremely cautious in dealing with white people. While on the one hand the teacher called to the students' attention the Logans' struggle for equality, he nevertheless appeared restricted in his own ability to empathise and understand the psychological reality of that struggle.

As mentioned previously, the teacher had other preoccupations absorbing his major energies by this stage and the kind of collaborative reflection for which I had hoped had not emerged. This was the first time he was teaching a work by a black author and he was neither very familiar with black writing nor issues of black experience. After an initially very positive response to the book, certain remarks he made later suggested a basic unease, for instance that it was 'wordy' and, surprisingly, that he thought Mildred Taylor must have been copying Harper Lee's *To Kill A Mockingbird* (1960) when writing because there were some similar incidents. He did not seem to recognise either the absurdity of implying that a black writer should need to copy from a white writer to describe black experience or that the experiences were not unique, but repeated thousands of time over in the South.

It was apparent by this time, in the middle of the spring term, that Alan was feeling increasingly irritated with the course. Although various factors were involved (including personal ones unrelated to the course), it could not be ignored that his irritation appeared to be mounting as the focus within the texts moved to a more specifically black/white domain. With his response at this point being one of retracting interest and continuing at a basically perfunctory level, I found myself unable to draw him out into acknowledging the problem and talking through the uncomfortable challenge of a black perspective.

Acknowledgement and exploration of white identity

Being able to explore one's own feelings and perceptions without becoming defensive is a pre-condition for being able to open out this area with students. It can only be done within a framework of trust. There were instances when, in the privacy of the reading journals and home tape recordings, some students not only indicated their consciousness of white identity but a sense of some disturbance. For example Neil —the boy who wrote in his journal that he was 'very proud of Jeremy' — also wrote how he admired Jeremy's persistence in trying to befriend the Logans and he wished that they would give him some encouragement. In an earlier comment he indicated 'I am also disappointed that the trouble starts at grass roots with the whites.'

Neil was not alone in acknowledging his white identity and expressing unease. Julia wrote 'I am very quickly beginning to hate whites and that includes me! The men are really cruel and it's a shame they have to have such an attitude as they have towards blacks.' Alison expressed her conflicting emotions about the racist attack on the Berry family — ending in death and burning — with particular honesty:

> 'How can any man do such a thing to another man?... I feel so angry and frustrated, when you know this kind of thing went on and the people responsible are the same colour as you. I feel guilty and responsible for their actions. And how can they just laugh about it? I just don't understand some people.'

Exploring this area would have required considerable sensitivity. The object of the students reading Mildred Taylor's novel was not for them to be left with a personal sense of white guilt or for them to 'hate whites'. What was important was for them to develop some understanding of the destructive effects of racism — not just in the physical sense, but in terms of the quality of relationships possible in a society in which a powerful element denies equality to, and oppresses, another section. It was important for them to begin to understand the damage to Jeremy as well as to Stacey Logan. It was important for them to begin to ask questions for themselves about racism.

An instance of this kind of genuine questioning could be heard coming from Alison in the discussion she taped at home with Erica. As with the tape they had made about *Friedrich* and the Holocaust, they moved beyond the initial set task. The students had been asked to respond to a number of reviewers' comments on *Roll Of Thunder, Hear My Cry* which appeared in the English Centre's background book. Having done this collaboratively at some length, Alison and Erica became involved in a more general discussion revolving around both the novel and the accompanying booklet. Alison seemed to have read more of the latter than had been specified by the teacher:

ERICA: And that's the kind of attitude they had wasn't it?

ALISON: Yeah where was it at? (looking through background book) There was something like 'Lynch her!'.. you know the way they hang them and that. They were willing to do that. I think that it is quite disgusting really.

ERICA: But it is stupid really the way they thought about them though wasn't it?

ALISON: Yeah I know.. but what I don't understand is why we felt this way towards them.

ERICA: They are no different are they?

> ALISON: No! That's what I can't understand. (Suppressed giggle from Erica — embarrassment?)

The critical feature in this interchange is Alison's switch from 'they' to 'we' in her statement about not understanding 'why we felt this way towards them'. While acknowledging both a common white identity — that what happened was connected in some way to her as a white person — and a sense of disgust, she expressed her incomprehension at the racist behaviour. Possibly it was the earnestness in Alison's tone that provoked Erica's giggle. Although close friends, Erica's comments in discussion and in writing never reflected the same kind of involvement as those of Alison. Alison's concern with understanding could be seen yet again in a final comment in her journal: 'Each child in the book is told at least once you are too young to understand. So how old do you have to be to understand?'

While Alison felt able to express her personal responses to Erica, as mentioned previously, she only spoke in class if directly called upon to do so. The fact that the classroom context was not sufficiently supportive to someone like Alison — so that she could feel confident to put forward her perceptions and concerns in a wider forum — was clearly a significant loss to the project. The implications of this are wide-reaching. While classrooms are obviously public places, if we want to gain the benefit of the kind of questions and sensitive responses offered by some students in more private forums, then we need to consider ways in which classrooms might be changed so these voices might be heard.

The students' perceptions of their own learning

In spite of the various limitations, final comments from the students suggested that quite a number perceived the novel as having had some effect on them. This was also despite initial difficulties with the dialogue. The majority of students, male and female, acknowledged that they had learnt things they had not known before about the extent of racism in the American South in the 1930s. Reviews by the girls, however, tended on the whole to be fuller and, in addition, to reveal more about an affective level of response.

There is an honesty and sensitivity in Gaby's final review which suggests a very real involvement with the text:

> 'I learned of family life in another country and the loving, caring thoughts they all have for each other. Also the other side where there is violence, bad feeling and a lot of unjust racism... I thought the book was very realistic and there was never a false word in it. I also learned of how children of my age or maybe a bit younger had to cope with lots of different problems. They seemed to understand more about many matters and also had a sense of humour and also a sense of fear and dignity and would always stand up for themselves no matter what the consequences may turn out to be. I think that I will never have the

same problems as they did and if I did I am not really sure how I would react but I don't think I would be as strong or stand up for myself as much as they did.'

Gaby's admiration for the Logans is evident, along with an awareness of how the conditions under which they lived — very different from her own — actually helped to create an admirable resilience and maturity in the children, which she sees lacking in herself. With this conceptual framework, Gaby in fact showed the potential to begin to explore issues of racism at a social and structural level, had this been encouraged.

A conversation with her close friend Jacky — whose response to the novel appeared frequently bound by a white perspective —provided a fascinating example of a non-confrontational mode of discussion by two speakers with different points of view. Having written in her journal that 'the book was very realistic and there was never a false word in it', Gaby nevertheless did not challenge Jacky when early on she questioned the novel's veracity:

> JACKY: I thought that the unity they (the Logans) had with each was a bit false.
>
> GABY: Yeah.

Shortly afterwards however when Gaby quietly made the assertion about the novel that 'it used to happen', Jacky sounded genuinely surprised, asking 'Did it?' But it was not long before Jacky's defensiveness began to surface a little more openly:

> JACKY: I think you know it was a bit unfair the way they said the whites had an easy life.. did you notice that? (GABY: Yeah) You know they were going they were really hard up and they had a really bad life and everything and the whites had an easy laid-back life... like they'd got money you know all the time.. but they had to work for that didn't they?
>
> GABY: Yeah.
>
> JACKY: I suppose they had it easier.. but if they had to work for it.. (pause) What's your opinion on that one?
>
> GABY: Well as I've already said, I think that the message although it is harsh, it's true.. (JACKY: Yeah) and you can't take it away really can you? You can't really say it wasn't true.
>
> JACKY: What do you think the message was then?
>
> GABY: (long pause) About survival and um.. how they coped, wasn't it?.. or maybe.. survival and how they coped with other people.. how they coped with the whites.

JACKY: Yeah.. I suppose so. I think the message was more saying that.. you know whites.. all whites have been really horrible to the blacks.. but they aren't nowadays, are they? I suppose they were. You know it was um like you've got to stick up for yourself and it's up to yourself to look after yourself.

GABY: Yeah mm.

JACKY: Yeah.

The use of 'yeah' by each girl should perhaps not be taken so much as a ratification of what the other has said, as much as simply an acknowledgement of the other person and her view. There seems to be the desire not to confront or argue. Gaby appeared still to hold on to the tenor of the responses expressed in her journal, although much more tentatively, hoping to gain the consensus of her friend. While Jacky did not directly deny Gaby's points she turned the focus to the white people, whom she claimed were all portrayed as 'horrible' and 'laid-back'. One might have expected Gaby, on the basis of what she had written in her journal, to question Jacky's interpretation. It is difficult to assess the extent to which she was aware of the apparent difference in their stated perspectives but simply not prepared to make an issue of it, for the sake of maintaining harmony. It is also interesting to note in this respect her journal comment about not being able to be 'as strong or stand up for myself' as the Logan children.

As with Gaby, Caroline's journal comments also revealed some self-reflection. Her sense of identification with the characters lead to her questioning her own ability to be as resistant and assertive as Cassie:

'I think I can identify with the characters more than any of the other books we have read in class. I can see myself in those positions and what I would have done would be a lot like Cassie... because the book was written so well I could picture myself in the positions of the characters at different times but if I was really black and I lived at that particular time I don't know what I would have done even though I agree with most things Cassie did I probably wouldn't have had the courage to do them. Before I read roll of thunder I didn't really know anything about slavery, now I know how everybody felt about it and what it really is.'

Here Caroline has made the distinction between imaginative identification within the realm of fiction and the reality of 'if I was really black'. The latter would in fact be difficult to imagine, given that her frames of reference had been constructed from experiences as a white child. However, as mentioned in relation to Gaby, Caroline's responses suggested the potential to begin exploring issues of social and structural racism and their effect on personal identity.

Caroline's comments indicated a qualitatively different response to the novel and its characters from that of Michelle, the girl expressing the most explicit racism on both Racist Perceptions Surveys. Her response to the Mildred Taylor video had been that it was 'sad really. This is because no-one liked the coloured children. They can't help it, they didn't choose to be coloured just like we didn't choose to be white'. Her response here was one of white sympathy and patronage. Her final review indicated her remaining firmly rooted in a white perspective, feeling however that she now knew more *'about* blacks' (my italics):

> 'From this book, I know much more about blacks. I hardly knew anything about them before, I never knew that the whites treated the blacks like that. From all the books we've read, I've learnt knew things which I didn't even know about... I think this book was really good, I liked it better than the others. It has taught me a lot about blacks.'

Michelle's acknowledgement of having enjoyed the novel and her sense of new learning seemed quite genuine. Nevertheless she clearly perceived this as learning about 'other' people. Her frames of reference appeared to remain fixed by a white vantage point. In the taped conversation between Michelle and her friend Hannah, much of the discussion reflected their concerns as young white people. For example:

> MICHELLE: I hardly knew anything about them really except that they were a different colour and that's all and now I know you know how the whites treated them and everything. But if I was a white in those times I don't know what I would have done.. if it was now you know..
>
> HANNAH: What if it was happening right now you would sort of probably identify with Jeremy? 'Cause of what he did?
>
> MICHELLE: Well I don't know whether I would identify with them you know.. go and hang around with them and everything but I wouldn't really treat them.. you know really bad.
>
> HANNAH: What even if everybody else did?
>
> MICHELLE: Well.. I don't know.
>
> HANNAH: I don't know what I'd do actually... because most people they sort of all follow the crowd in a way don't they?
>
> MICHELLE: Yeah.. um..
>
> HANNAH: I mean unless you are sort of a born leader then you can sort of do what you want..

Neither girl raised the question of racism from the perspective of the Logans. Instead they focused on how they might respond as white people, with

Hannah appearing ready to exonerate complicity in racism with the notion of most people being powerless to make their own decisions with the exception of the 'born leader'.

Amongst the boys, two very clear examples of students suggesting they had gained new 'knowledge' while continuing to display fixed racist perceptions were provided by John and Ian (the two highest scorers on both Racist Perceptions Surveys). John first focused on the book's 'moral' for racists, before revealing in his next sentence his own deeply racist perceptions and fears about black people:

> 'I think that Roll of Thunder was quite a strong book and it would teach racist people quiet a lot in that black etc. are exactly the same as themselves. It makes me think that if it could happen in the 1930s it could happen now, which is frightening really as it could be that blacks try to do it.'

John — who on a number of occasions qualified what he said with statements like 'I'm not being racist but..' — often seemed concerned to say the 'right' thing. It is difficult to know how conscious were his attempts to cover up racist feelings. It was my personal feeling that Ian was frequently more consciously manipulative in what he said and wrote than John. With the increasing focus on black-white relations in the course, there appeared to be a growing undertone of resentment in Ian's journal comments. At times there seemed also to be a hint of callousness, possibly calculated to provoke. His bored prediction at the beginning that *Roll of Thunder, Hear My Cry* 'is just like discrimination between whites and blacks' was followed by contradictory messages in response to the white bus driver's attack on the Logan children. While apparently condemning it on the one hand, he casually stated that some discrimination against black people was inevitable. The suggestion was that the bus driver was perhaps just going a bit over the top:

> 'I think it's wrong just because of the colour. The worst thing is when the bus came by and everybody signalled horrible things and especially an adult encouraging them... I think that blacks are blacks and they are bound to get some stick but this is very much cruel and I wouldn't want to be on the white bus if that happened.'

Ian's implicit attitude appeared to be that black people should simply accept their station in life. After reading about the treatment of the children by the white shopkeeper during Mama's trip to sell her produce in Strawberry, he wrote:

> 'if people are going to hate them all there live I can't seen them bothering to try and sell there dairy produce... I think the part where the shop keeper is serving other [white] people whilst serving T.J. is just stressing a point which we already no. Whites don't like blacks.'

Ian's tone implied 'So what?'. His written comments seemed to match his body language and deliberately casual manner of speaking at times — a tactic which appeared to be aimed at subverting serious attention away from the topic under discussion. Writing about the tragedy of T.J., he not only contradicted himself but appeared to be wanting to shock:

> 'I think they should let him get what is coming to him and death I don't think will teach him anything. They should set an example to everybody else and give him a slow death I think that way will make him think He will then know that his life has been squandered. So far the book has been nothing special..'

In his final review, written shortly after the above, Ian once again — while saying on the one hand that the work had been 'very good fun' — conveyed more fundamentally a sense of bored superiority:

> 'I think the work we have done connected with roll of thunder has been very good fun and I have learnt that the blacks were treated very harshly. I didn't think that they were treated quite as badly as the book made out. I knew that the blacks and whites didn't like each other but I didn't know they went to extremes to hurt each other... I knew most of what they were telling me. The blacks are a subject which we regularly hear about and are common knowledge so I didn't find it as knowledgeable as Friedrich was. I would give the book 8/10.'

The disparagement is clear. The question has to be asked whether for a student like Ian — whose racist frames of reference were deeply entrenched — the net result of studying *Roll of Thunder, Hear My Cry* was not simply to produce a better-informed racist? Such a pessimistic interpretation, however, should be qualified by reminding ourselves that the outcome, even for a student like Ian, may have been different had the teacher's awareness of racism been deeper and the teacher more committed to engaging with students' responses from an anti-racist perspective.

In contrast to Ian, Neil's view about the potential of the novel to change perceptions might seem idealistic when generalised but is nevertheless instructive about his own thinking. In a tape made alone at home he stated:

> 'The book gives us a bigger view... and helps us develop new ways of thinking. If someone was quite racist then it would, I think, help them to think in different ways.. how the trouble started, how it developed and why blacks were campaigning so much for equal rights because a racist person might think they were just doing it for the sake of it.. nothing better to do than go and bother the government. This book helps to break down that way of thinking. I would recommend it to be read in schools.'

Neil's focus was on rationality and the power of rational argument 'to break down' a racist 'way of thinking'. This is an extremely important perspective, showing an awareness of historical understanding. Yet while acknowledging that the book 'has opened up a whole new channel of knowledge about the slavery in the South of America', Neil could not understand why Cassie so resented having to apologise to Jeremy's malicious sister Lillian Jean for not getting off the pavement to make way for her. It is interesting to speculate what prevented Neil from making affective identification with Cassie at that point. It is also another reminder of the complexity of our responses as readers.

Like Neil, Michael similarly believed that the book should be widely read:

> 'This book should be read in all schools because it teaches people about how the blacks were persecuted and a lot of people are in the dark and it's important they should know what the blacks went through at this time.'

In his own responses to the novel Michael did not hold back in referring to his own emotions. For instance, in his final review he wrote how 'The last few lines touched me where Cassie told us that she never liked T.J. but what had happened swayed her thoughts... It was very enjoyable'. The last sentence suggested however that his emotions remained fairly comfortable, rather than disturbed. In contrast to Neil's focus on reason, Michael felt the novel would change the feelings of readers, although he did not indicate how:

> '...because those people who like blacks already, this will make them like blacks more and perhaps the people that don't like blacks very much, having read some of the situations that have happened in this book will make them like them after all because many people that don't like blacks don't even know why. I've heard people that don't like blacks say 'I don't like the black people and I've asked them why and they haven't a clue'.'

Whereas Neil thought analytically in terms of developing understanding of the process and effects of discrimination, Michael conceptualised the problem of attitude in sweepingly simple terms of either liking or not liking black people. His tone of voice on the tape was sincere and it was as if he was genuinely thinking out his responses on the spot. However it is worth recalling that on the two Racist Perceptions Surveys Michael scored in the medium-high range, on both occasions registering himself as uncertain about having more black students in school, having a family of another colour move next door and unsure about black-white marriages. In other words, a sympathetic response to *Roll of Thunder, Hear My Cry* appeared not to shift these fundamentally racist perceptions or, in his own simplistic terms, make him 'like blacks more'.

Probably the most emotive final response amongst the boys came from Paul, who not only acknowledged strong emotions but wrote of 'a new perspective' having developed within himself:

> 'This story was powerful and sad. quite clearly one of the most brilliant books I've ever read... This book has given me a new perspective of how blacks were treated. I think the books we've read have given everybody a new perspective of races being treated poorly.'

Here again a student has generalised the effects of the novel. Having made a very positive and significant statement about his own sense of personal change, Paul assumes that others too would have gained 'a new perspective'. The reality appeared to be rather that those students who were already tending to openness were the ones most open to Mildred Taylor's messages. For Angela, it was 'brilliant!!!!! the best book I have read at St Mary's' and in discussion with her friend Tanya, she recorded her own process of discovery as a reader responsive to where she was being placed by the writer:

> ANGELA: Cassie learns about her generation and the generation before her and all her ancestors being slaves.. and when they take you back on their journey it's like us learning as well as if you're in Cassie's place.

Angela's metaphor of learning through the narrative as a journey has considerable potential. We might start our journey at different points, travel for different lengths, and indeed see different things on the way. Those students who were most ready for the journey with Cassie perhaps travelled further, observing, experiencing and reflecting the most. Nevertheless the evidence of the students' responses suggested that many of them embarked on the journey for at least some of the way.

Chapter Six

Shifting perspectives across the 'race' divide in South Africa — responses to Waiting for the Rain

Outline of '*Waiting for the Rain*' and related activities

Sheila Gordon's first novel for young people focuses on the relationship of two boys — one white, one black — growing up in South Africa around the 1980s. Frikkie sees himself destined to inherit his uncle's farm with all its privileges. He assumes that Tengo — his childhood playmate, son of the foreman and the housemaid — will simply follow in his father's footsteps to become Frikkie's own 'boss-boy' when they are grown up. While Frikkie chafes at the constraints of school, Tengo is consumed with questions about the wider world. But, to Frikkie's uncle, education for his workers' children would just cause trouble, giving them ideas above their station.

It is through his cousin Joseph from Soweto that Tengo first begins to reflect on the condition of his life. Joseph's mother works for a family of white liberals in Johannesburg, the Millers, about whom Joseph becomes increasingly cynical. When Tengo eventually manages to leave the farm to attend school in Soweto, Dr. Miller offers to pay for his books. Joseph points out to Tengo that the cost is probably less than the annual fees for the golf club. It is too late for benevolent goodwill by whites who envisage no actual change in their own lifestyle. What is required is a transfer of actual power to address the legacy of oppression.

With Soweto going up in flames, Tengo is faced first with a bitter conflict of whether to join the student boycotts or concentrate solely on his studies, and later of whether to join Joseph in the underground African National Congress by crossing the border to go for educational or military training. Frikkie, by this time a conscript in the South African Army, looks forward to the day when he can leave dealing with troublesome 'kaffirs' for the peace of farm life. Almost inevitably, the author brings Frikkie and Tengo together for a final confrontation. For the first time Tengo speaks his mind to an uncomprehending Frikkie, confronting him with his complicity in a system designed to destroy all reasonable expectations of life for those who are not white.

The novel seems to me to have a two-fold strength. The structure is one designed to keep shifting the reader from one boy's perspective to the other's. While the book begins through Frikkie's eyes, the reader is increasingly shifted into Tengo's consciousness — the structure thus reflecting Tengo's increasing awareness, contrasted sharply with Frikkie's psychological blindness. The second strength is that most of the white protagonists are not portrayed as intrinsically mean or unpleasant. Racism is thus not located in personal individual characteristics. It is located firmly in a system which gives one group unbridled power over another. As in the two previous novels, there is the potential to explore dimensions of racism beyond those of personal attitude. I felt, for instance, that an attempt to understand Joseph's perspective on the friendly, liberal Millers would indicate the potential to perceive this fundamental dimension of power. Would the difficulties which students had experienced in understanding the Logans' wariness of Jeremy in *Roll of Thunder, Hear My Cry* also be reflected here in a feeling that Joseph was being too harsh on the Millers, and Tengo too harsh on Frikkie at the end of the novel?

Prior to reading *Waiting for the Rain*, the students attended an activity-based science session on classification, aimed at encouraging them to question the notion of 'race' as a scientific biological construct. They discussed a documentary on apartheid and 'race' classification (BBC 1988) and also read *Journey to Jo'burg* while I was away, without being aware that I was the author. Apart from journal writing and responses to specific passages and issues, later activities included comparing two versions of South African history; viewing *Girls Apart* (Sheppard and Sauvageot 1987), a documentary on two South African sixteen-year-olds — one black, one white; and discussing a taped interview I had done with Sheila Gordon, author of *Waiting for the Rain*. In drama the focus continued on issues of status and power, through developing the role play of inter-school conflict. The final drama sessions were however focused more directly on wider social issues relating to migration from the Caribbean to Britain.

Language and power
Waiting for the Rain is a rich resource for exploring the role of language in relation to power. In particular, the novel offers a way in to feeling the effect

of derogatory classifications. An interesting example of this was provided by Michelle. Her initial response to the novel on the basis of its cover suggested a certain distance: 'It's about blacks and whites again! We seem to be doing a lot about them.' However, by the third chapter she was revealing involvement:

> 'I think it's not fair that Tengo should be only boss-boy. Boss-boy will probably be the same as what he is now. When Frikkie owns the farm... Tengo and him won't get on at all. Tengo won't like the way Frikkie bosses him about, and they'll probably turn into enemies... Tengo has obviously got his skill for clay from his ancestors — I think his tribe were on the land first, and the whites came in immediately and took it over.'

Michelle's response here seemed to be grounded in a sense of unfairness and a strong reaction against 'bossing'. This could be seen in her reaction against Frikkie's sister Sissie who 'thinks she's the boss' and their red-haired girl cousin who spoke rudely to the old servant Ezekiel:

> 'I thought it was a real cheek for that girl to call Ezekiel an old man — boy. Tengo was furious and I would've been as well.'

Later on in her journal Michelle returned to the issue of names, commenting on the use of language for purposes of power:

> 'Tengo's aunt is called a 'tea-girl'. I don't see why she can't be called a 'tea-lady', it is just like when the red haired girl called Ezekiel 'boy'. I think it's because adults have power over children by calling them boy and girl. But adults don't have power over adults. So I think for the white people to feel they have power they call blacks by boy and girl. I think it gives them satisfaction for now they can have power by calling the blacks this.'

Michelle is attempting here to internalise the argument about how language can be used as a means of oppression, following a brief class discussion led by the teacher on the effect of using the terms 'boy' and 'girl'. She is beginning to grapple with important and difficult ideas for herself. She is of course not correct in thinking that adults do not have power over other adults or that the actual basis of adults' power over children lies in 'calling them boy and girl' — the implication being that the power is manufactured simply by the use of language. Tengo's aunt was called 'girl' and the old man Ezekiel called 'boy' — even by a white child — because the white community had effective power over them. Nevertheless language is also a crucial part of the process of constructing power. Both white and black children hearing black adults referred to as 'boy' and 'girl' learn about the power relationships in the society. Black adults forced to use the demeaning terminology when referring to other black adults, in conversation with white 'masters' and 'mistresses', are involuntarily involved in sustaining the power relationships through language. Thus apart from helping students discover how language is indeed a function of power, we need to enable them to explore how language also helps construct perceptions of power and serves to preserve it.

While the issue of language was one which clearly captured Michelle's attention, most of the students did not make any comment in their journals and would have benefited from a more concentrated focus on language and power in ways that actively drew on their own experience. Responses to the word 'kaffir' suggested that more was needed than a general class discussion to deconstruct its meaning and function. In the early part of the book, the word 'kaffir' is used by Frikkie's family as a normal term of reference for black people. It is only when Frikkie's uncle shouts at Tengo 'you lazy kaffir' (Chapter 5) that his tone directly reveals abuse. The teacher deliberately delayed discussing the word until this point in the text, where the contempt was explicit rather than implicit and the reader was clearly meant to be placed with Tengo at the point of impact. In the class discussion and subsequent journal comments, a number of students revealed that they had been unaware of the word's abusive connotations until that point. For instance, Alison who was always extremely sensitive wrote:

> 'The word 'Kaffir' I hadn't thought of it as being an abusive word until now when the oubaas shouted at Tengo. I thought it was just a harmless word but I definately think in this incident it is meant abusively.'

Although Alison placed the word 'kaffir' in quotation marks, it was disconcerting to find a number of students using the word without them. In a previous response sheet connected with *Roll of Thunder, Hear My Cry* the students' attention had been drawn specifically to the function of quotation marks in relation to the word 'nigger', yet not all the students had followed the injunction to use them. In most cases where students used the word 'kaffir' it was when writing about white perceptions, for example

> 'I think Oom Koos was being really racist when he says that no kaffirs could ever work any type of machinery well' (Tanya).

> 'the whites say the kaffirs brake machinery' (Peter).

It was my feeling that neither Tanya nor Peter actually wanted to identify with the contempt implicit in 'kaffir' and that they and other students needed to be involved in more specific 'knowledge about language' activity in order to learn how to use quotation marks as a distancing mechanism. The class discussion on the word focused on the speaker's intention and the context in which a particular word is used — for instance whether it is possible ever to use a word like 'Paki' without it being offensive. However I felt it would have required more time and active participation for the students to be able really to grasp the issues. In addition, although the teacher had a specific reason for delaying the discussion, in the meantime the word 'kaffir' may well have been gaining a kind of legitimacy. Andrew, with his South African experience, acknowledged in discussion that he had been aware the word was abusive from the beginning. Indeed I had seen him grinning whenever it had come up in the text and he had used the word with what seemed to be a certain relish in a group discussion on 'race' classification. I felt the same pleasure was evident in his substitution of 'nigger' for 'kaffir' when later in his journal he wrote that Frikkie's uncle 'feels that niggers are not better than a white and the only way to teach them is by force.'

Another student who seemed to be deliberately using the term 'kaffir' was Ian. I already felt Ian was increasingly intent on disparaging things that were challenging his racist frames of reference. By the third chapter of *Waiting for the Rain* he had written 'The book is already starting to dwell on black and white hardships. This subject is starting to drag on and get very boring.' His comment after the discussion of 'kaffir' once again revealed his skill at casual contempt: 'when the word kaffirs is used it's read offensively like it is for one of your niggers.' Had Ian been asked to spell out what he meant by 'one of your niggers', I suspect he would have been elusive, insisting that he was referring to someone else's terminology and not his own. However he continued to repeat the term 'kaffir' as if it was a word in normal usage, despite commenting that 'All the way through the book kaffir has changed its meaning from light-hearted to insulting.' His conception of 'kaffir' being used initially in a 'light-hearted' way was revealing and would seem to link with his notion expressed elsewhere that racist jokes were 'just a bit of fun'. For a student like Ian, seeing racist language in print probably provided extra scope for articulating his own racism while providing the 'cover' that he was simply using words from the text.

The question of handling racist terminology within literature is a difficult one for a teacher, where there is no immediate counter to it within the text. In *Roll of Thunder, Hear My Cry* the shop-keeper's insult 'Whose little nigger is this?' receives an instant retort from Cassie 'I ain't nobody's little nigger!' (Chapter 5). The reader is also clearly placed with Cassie on the receiving — and therefore rejecting — end of the abuse. However the structure of *Waiting for the Rain* means that the reader has a shifting perspective, sometimes hearing the racist abuse without there being an immediate critique. Is it sufficient for the teacher to wait until the abuse is countered later within the text — for instance, when the reader is taken into Tengo's perspective, and specifically at the end of the book when Tengo confronts Frikkie with his acceptance of the term 'kaffir', amongst all the other injustices he has simply accepted? Should the teacher not attempt, without becoming didactic, to enable the students to be critically aware of the connotations of the abuse at the time it occurs? Although there may be little chance of affecting a student with such marked racist frames of reference as Ian, this approach would at least not imply a kind of legitimacy for the abuse through lack of comment.

The project students did in fact become actively involved in deconstructing bias when they undertook the exercise comparing two versions of South African history. This was linked to the section in the novel where Tengo listens to Frikkie's uncle tell his Afrikaner version of the 'Great Trek'. The students were first given a page of a text in which South Africa's history begins with 'discovery' by Europeans, portrayed very positively in terms of 'settling' and 'building' the country. In contrast the country's indigenous black inhabitants are portrayed as 'wandering' around, prone to fighting the Europeans, and generally being a 'problem'. Alan Parsons read the passage in a straight tone before asking whether it seemed a reasonable account. While a couple of students commented that the text was perhaps a bit simplified and Jacky said that it 'sounds a bit one-sided', no-one strongly contested that the text might be biased or contain anything untrue. They were then given another text to read — one specifically written by the black writer Chris van Wyk (1986) to counter the white perspective which has predominated in historical accounts for children.

Initial responses from a few students indicated that they felt the second passage told them more about what really happened. In the class discussion which followed, students began to point out omissions and distortions in the first piece. There was a focus for instance on the difference between saying that South Africa was 'discovered' and that it was 'invaded'. When the teacher finally revealed that the passage being criticised for its distortion was from the *Children's Encyclopedia Britannica*, in as recent an edition as 1985, there was obvious surprise, the strongest reaction being voiced by Angela. The teacher allocated a further session for the students to work in pairs, looking more closely for evidence of bias within the language, and both he and I felt these language-focused sessions were very productive.

Given more time, this kind of work could have been extended to more explicit considerations of language and power and questions about whose versions of history predominate and how young people are generally inducted into an 'accepted' version. What was needed was time and space for students to reflect on how their own perceptions were being constructed by the language around them and the language they themselves used.

Student responses to criticism of the white liberals

As indicated earlier, I was particularly interested to find out about how students would respond to Joseph's critique of the liberal Miller family as well as to the conflict between Frikkie and Tengo. In the first passage from the text to which they were asked to make a specific response, Joseph remains silent when his mother clearly expects him to thank her white 'Madam' for paying for his train ticket, after being sent to recuperate after an illness on the farm where his cousin Tengo lived. The white woman's manner is benevolent and the author subtly signifies the power relationship behind the affability. For example Mrs Miller complains of the heat in the kitchen because of the oven and asks Joseph's mother, Matilda, to bring her a tray of tea by the swimming pool. Matilda's place is, of course, to remain at work in the kitchen. The students were asked to write Joseph's thoughts at this point, so eliciting an indication of how sensitive they were to his inner resentment.

Once again the gender difference in responses appeared rather striking. Only a third of the boys showed some recognition of Joseph's growing sense of injustice and only one boy (Carl) identified these feelings as Joseph's major pre-occupation at this point. In sharp contrast more than four-fifths of the girls indicated understanding, most of them also showing sympathy for how Joseph was feeling.

A couple of students openly expressed the view that the Millers deserved gratitude from Joseph. Amongst the girls Jacky seemed distinctly unsympathetic to Joseph's feelings. In the thought-tracking exercise, she felt Joseph's silence revealed jealousy: his mother was 'taking more notice of 'Madam' than of him and was more concerned about Tengo getting a box of books from the Millers instead of giving all her attention to her son. In her subsequent journal comment Jacky wrote: 'I thought Joseph was very ungreatful to the Millers he may be jealous of them.'

Dan, too, regarded Joseph as rather ungrateful and 'selfish':

> 'I feel quite hardened by the thought of blacks having bad conditions to travel in but even worse, its because of my race... It was very kind of Madam to give Tengo some books. Matilda is quite lucky not to have racist Masters. I think that at the end of this chapter Joseph was becoming a bit selfish by not thanking his mother's Master for paying his train fare.'

On the surface there appeared to be some contradiction in Dan's responses. On the one hand he recognised 'bad conditions' for black people — and somehow felt implicated because he was white — but he couldn't understand Joseph's resentment since his 'Madam' and 'Master' were 'kind'. However these responses are reconcilable within a conception of racism concerned purely with personal attitudes and not to do with social structures. Dan did not relate the Millers to the 'bad conditions' because they were 'kind' and not 'racist Masters'. In that way presumably he could deal with the uncomfortable feelings within himself and distance himself from what he identified as racism i.e. the 'bad conditions' for black people which would have been the fault of unkind racists. This locating of racism solely in individuals who specifically articulate racist ideas seemed to be borne out elsewhere in Dan's journal e.g.

> 'The postmistress is a racist person and I'm surprised that Oom Koos [Frikkie's uncle] didn't say anything...

'Sissie seems like a spoilt brat and is fussy about everything. She also seems to be quite a racist person.'

Dan did not appear to see how all the white characters were locked into a racist system, regardless of personality. Although he occasionally showed glimmerings of understanding, he did not follow these through. While writing 'I'm beginning to see how, in this book, there is a distinct seperation in equality between blacks and whites', he did not seem able — or willing — to take on the implications. When Tengo's ambition to get his matric was thwarted by the student protests, Dan was unable to combine his sympathy for Tengo with an understanding of the school boycotters' perspective. To him they were 'selfish because their forcing children to finish school with nothing. No certificates for their exams. When all this boycotting is over, what will happen to the kids who couldn't do their matric and they need a job.' This unwillingness to recognise the wider social ramifications of racism — and therefore the need for wider social action to dismantle it — was not limited to Dan. Locating racism in society has far more uncomfortable implications for everyone than simply locating it in certain individuals.

A few students did however appear to confront themselves with Joseph's view of the Millers. Alison wrote very honestly: 'I never saw it from Joseph's point of view they were white liberals but when Joseph said about the golf club I had to think again about the Millers.' There was also an interesting example of a student showing empathy with the young Joseph in the 'thought-tracking' exercise (carried out in class) but then indicating more reserve in her subsequent journal comment (for homework). In writing Joseph's thoughts, Gaby imagined him to be strongly resentful of oppression:

> 'How come they have got so much money anyway I don't want to have anything to do with them. How do they know that I want to say thank-you for the train ticket it is always the same us people having to lick the boots of other people and except charity... That Madam seems very bossy and always likes her own way she might be very nice to give books to Tengo but she proably always thinks of herself first and if anyone needs to go for a swim my mother does. she has been working all day over a hot stove...'

In her journal comment however Gaby revealed a certain conflict:

> 'To me I thought or I had a good opinion of the Millers but for the same reason Joseph has got something against them or maybe he is just jealous because of the money.'

I should have liked to have been able to ask Gaby to think through her conflicting feelings in relation to the Millers and not evade the problem by reducing Joseph's response simply to one of jealousy, when she already knew it to be much more complex. It is particularly at points like this that one can see the value of running a journal system which allows for a private dialogue between student and teacher. I should have wished also to be able to ask Louise to probe further into the duality she expressed in: 'I suppose Dr Miller is a reasonable kind person to work for... but he believes that he has a right to have black servants.'

Only one student explicitly suggested the Millers' attitudes and perspective might have something to do with power:

> 'I think that the whites who Joseph's mother works for must have some good reason for paying for their books and education, maybe if the blacks rise to power over whites they can't get treated badly.'

Perhaps Peter's conception of the Millers was simplistic and somewhat Machiavellian, denying any genuine humanitarian feelings on their part. Nevertheless he touched on the concept of power.

The teacher and the white liberals

It seemed to me that a number of students had the potential to break out from a conception of racism as confined to a matter of personal hostility. Given the right challenges and the space to explore the issues, I felt there were students who might have come to an understanding that the English Millers, like Frikkie's Afrikaner family, could not escape the moral implications of benefiting from a system of inequality and racist power. However, in the class discussion about Joseph's view of the Millers, Alan Parsons focused almost entirely on the white perspective. He began by asking the students 'What's your attitude towards his [Joseph's] attitude towards the white liberals?'

When there was no immediate response he elaborated by asking them how they would feel about 'the Millers' nice home being turned over to a public building of some sort.' Responses to this included that 'it would be vandalised' (Philip) and that 'it would be like what the Nazis did to the Jews' (Marco). When Jacky proposed that it would not work out because too many people would want the houses and there would not be the money to keep them up, the teacher asked what the Bolsheviks had done to private property in Russia. With Angela speaking about how 'they let it out to everybody.. everybody started living in it' and Michael declaring that the rich houses had been smashed up in the rebellion so there was nothing left, Graham brought the discussion back to South Africa:

> GRAHAM: That's what the blacks will do.. destroy it, smash the windows and things.
>
> A.P.: You think that will be a bad thing?
>
> GRAHAM: Yes.

A.P.: How do you think the Millers would feel if they were listening to this conversation?

GRAHAM: I think they'd feel angry because the blacks don't realise that they are actually trying to help them in some ways and they just think that they don't do anything.

A.P.: They'd be angry because it's not showing any sensitivity to them trying to help?

IAN: After all they've done for them, they'd be a bit sort of shocked that they would do it back to them.

A.P.: Miranda?

MARION: They'd probably stop helping them because they would think they were going to go down with all the others.

Instead of Joseph's speech being used to explore his expression of frustration and oppression, the teacher used it solely to open out white fears about revolution. He neither offered nor elicited from the students any critique of these, for instance not even questioning the statement that 'it'll be like what the Nazis did to the Jews'. From the focus he created it would appear that he himself felt strong sympathy with the Millers and little with Joseph at this point. Once again, as in *Roll of Thunder, Hear My Cry*, the teacher appeared constricted by an essentially white, albeit liberal, perspective. He too was bound into the Millers' paternalism and was unable to encourage the students to see beyond it.

Responses towards the novel's central black and white characters

In the final chapter of the novel Frikkie and Tengo confront each other as young men — Frikkie as a soldier and Tengo as a student protester. Frikkie is injured and for the first time in Tengo's life their positions of power are temporarily reversed. Tengo uses the opportunity to tell Frikkie what he really thinks. In order to discover how the students perceived the conflict, they were asked to stop reading just before the author's resolution of the crisis and to write a personal statement both to Tengo and to Frikkie indicating any support or criticism. These statements — only some of which were written directly in the first person to each character — provided a clear picture of where the students' sympathies lay at that point.

In broad terms, apart from two girls whose sympathies seemed fairly evenly divided, all the girls present supported Tengo rather than Frikkie. However most included some minor qualifications which I shall discuss later. In striking contrast, less than a third of the boys shared this perspective, with a third clearly feeling closer to Frikkie and a couple feeling rather divided. The remaining boys gave the impression of being undecided.

The student offering the most straightforward support to Frikkie was Andrew, the boy who had lived in South Africa and defended apartheid in the group discussion about 'race' classification. Not only was his support unqualified but he added a couple of traditional white South African justifications for racist supremacy:

> 'Tengo is being unfair to Frikkie. I think that if the whites didn't take Africa the blacks would probably still be fighting and wouldn't have gone forwards in technology... Frikkie and the whites should be worried because there are more blacks than whites.'

It is worth recalling that Andrew scored towards the non-racist end of the scale of Racist Perceptions, indicating either his ability to cover up views he identified as 'unacceptable' to teachers, or that the survey simply didn't tap in to his particular forms of racist thinking.

In the previous lesson's class discussion, Ian had shown strong sympathy for Frikkie, speaking about his being 'trapped' by not being allowed to gain his own knowledge. Such a statement seemed to have potential for learning. If he was able to see Frikkie as someone whose perceptions were largely constructed for him, perhaps this could lead to questioning of how his own views might have been shaped. In the group discussion on 'race classification' he had also spoken of young people being confused by conflicting adult conceptions. However, while I would have expected Ian to show support for Frikkie in this final conflict, his response was quite enigmatic:

> 'I think that I'm drawn towards Tengo and what I would say to him is urge him on and make him hate Frikkie so much that he killed him. I wouldn't say anything at all to Frikkie because I think he is still dreaming and doesn't even know what reality is.'

Did Ian simply write this provocatively as a 'send up', in order to create deliberate ambiguity? It is difficult to find another explanation.

John was quite open in his support for Frikkie:

> 'To Frikkie: Frikkie don't give up. you want that farm and its rightly yours. you couldn't help what happened between black and whites... don't you see he's just trying to get at you but don't let him. stand up for yourself. he hit you!

> 'To Tengo: Tengo ease of abit alright so he was blind in seeing about how you got treated on the farm. well your going of to another country aren't you. if you can't have it why should you not let Frikkie get it your being abit selfish!'

A number of boys suggested that the discrimination against Tengo was not Frikkie's fault. Their reasoning was reminiscent of that given mainly by boys in exonerating the narrator's parents from responsibility for the outcomes of Nazism in *Friedrich*. Tony, for instance, wrote:

'I feel sympathetic to Frikkie, because its not his fault that he has to do these things [in the army] I think that just because Tengo has learnt about these new things, he feels angered to any white person. Frikkie seems to be enclosed by Tengo's anger. I think that some of Tengo's statements are true.'

Tony appeared to credit the truth of at least some of what Tengo was saying but once again, the problem seemed to be acknowledging how someone like Frikkie was not simply an individual but inextricably linked with his society. Philip's attitude shared some similarity, judging from his statement that Frikkie did not make the laws:

'I would tell Tengo not to be so hard on Frikkie because Frikkie didn't make the laws and Tengo thinks he is a victim but in a way Frikkie is a victim as well because of the way he has to go to school but Tengo dosn't have to. And Frikkie has to do military service but Tengo dosn't.'

Philip's notion of Frikkie as a victim because of having to go to school appeared grounded in a child's perspective. He was clearly not thinking of Frikkie as a victim of a racist system in the sense that the human relationships open to those from the oppressor class are severely constricted. This probably involved a degree of abstraction difficult for most fourteen year olds to grasp.

Over a third of the students, both boys and girls, including those largely sympathetic to Tengo, spoke of him 'over-reacting', going a bit 'over the top' or being a bit 'petty', 'selfish' or 'unreasonable'. Given the author's depiction of Tengo as extremely reflective and restrained, this seemed to indicate something significant about the students' own frames of reference:

'Tengo is right in what he said to Frikkie, but I think he is going a bit over the top. It is not all Frikkie's fault the way he was brought up, so I think he believes what he was taught when he was younger... Tengo had been unfair in some of the things he said, but Frikkie still didn't relise some things.' (Michelle)

'I think that Tengo is being a bit unreasonable expecting Frikkie to understand, but I think that Frikkie is stuborn, he could try to understand. I think I would back up everything Tengo has said... You expect Frikkie to defend himself and stick up for his people, but he doesn't understand how Tengo's people feel and how they are treated.' (Louise)

'Tengo should cool down a bit. He is trying to say alot of his problems about whites to Frikkie but he shouldn't be saying it is his fault all the time, although it's the people like Frikkie that Tengo really hates...

Tengo is being a little bit petty but he has got reason too. I would tend to take Tengo's side.' (Caroline)

In these examples, it could be seen how even students supportive of Tengo felt it necessary to balance a view in which the criticism fell heavily on Frikkie for having participated in an oppressive system. As an individual Frikkie is clearly a friendly, sympathetic character but the author asks us to acknowledge that a warm, attractive individual can at the same time participate in perpetuating an oppressive society. Indeed that is the tragedy of the relationship between Tengo and Frikkie. Without the inequality they could have been good friends. An essential factor for grasping this idea is the concept of how an individual is at the same time part of a society in which she or he plays a role. It was my feeling that many students saw Frikkie and Tengo only as individuals. Instead of being able to acknowledge the tragedy of Frikkie's involvement in the system oppressing Tengo, they remained fixed on interpreting the relationship on a purely personal level. In those terms Tengo was being unfair to blame Frikkie. This way of viewing the relationship between the two protagonists bore a strong resemblance to how the relationship between the Logan children and Jeremy in *Roll of Thunder, Hear My Cry* was generally conceived — without a proper appreciation of the dimension of power which unavoidably separated the two parties.

Nevertheless the students sympathetic to Tengo showed the potential to develop a wider social understanding, had there been the direction and space to explore the issues further. Amongst the students themselves were those who touched on questions about Frikkie's responsibility as a member of an oppressive society. Erica, for instance, seemed to be pointing to the fact that Tengo and Frikkie were more than individuals, fulfilling certain social roles:

'I would back Tengo but he did go abit far in some places. Frikkie however didn't understand one bit of what Tengo was saying. 'Violence is caused by the law' Tengo had said. 'I don't make the law' Frikkie replied but he is keeping it (law) is what I would say to Frikkie. If they changed around then I bet Frikkie would put in exactly the same argument as Tengo is and Tengo would put in the same as Frikkie is.'

A particularly interesting response came from Peter who showed himself torn between Frikkie and Tengo as individuals. Furthermore he indicated his awareness of a feeling from some of the class as well as the teacher that Tengo was being 'too harsh' on Frikkie. Nevertheless he raised for himself an important question about responsibility and age:

'I've found it hard to go on either side with Tengo or Frikkie because of their faults or understanding. Like Frikkie didn't understand a lot of what was being said even at twenty, so I find this his fault. So I am tending to go on Tengo's side a lot more but even so Mr. Parsons and some of the class said Tengo was being too harsh on Frikkie with not understanding. But I think seeing their both about twenty it's no excuse for Frikkie not to understand.'

Angela also addressed the issue of 'harshness', expressing the view that 'I think Tengo is right in nearly all he says and although he is harsh he needs to be because Frikkie can't see what's happening... he is right when he says that the land belongs to all those who live in it black or white.'

Another student who, like Peter, directly confronted the question not only of her feelings but of Frikkie's responsibility was Alison. Her responses to *Waiting for the Rain*, as with the other novels, were fulsome and honest. In the course of the novel she continually challenged herself to think through the issues, recording not neat and tidy thoughts but the various ways in which her responses were pulling her. On a number of occasions for instance she returned to the question of violence, noting that 'Even though I don't like violence I think I would fight for freedom.' Earlier on in the novel she had commented that Frikkie reminded her sometimes of Jeremy, adding that 'I feel quite sorry for Frikkie sometimes, the same way I felt sorry for Jeremy.' By the final chapter, however, after increasingly experiencing Tengo's perspective, the complexity of her responses had deepened considerably:

'I'm glad Tengo hit him over the head maybe it will knock some sense into him. Frikkie did have a choice he didn't have to join the army he could have gone to another country or help the black people. I think Tengo is right, I don't think he's being too hard on Frikkie, I think he deserves everything he gets. 'We're not to blame' well if they are not to blame who is? If I was Tengo I would feel angry like him, I would also say all those things. Tengo is the one with power now not Frikkie. It's got everything to do with Frikkie. I don't know how Frikkie couldn't have noticed the difference in the plates. What sort of things have the white people done that are good? In my opinion nothing, well there might be some white people who should be given credit for trying to help. I think Tengo is hoping too much because I don't think that the black people will take over the country completely. Frikkie seems very frightened, not that I care. I don't think Tengo hates Frikkie. I think Tengo threw the rocks etc. to let out his anger and hate. The amount of soldiers killed is about 3 to every 100 of black people killed. What I'd say to Tengo would be to help Frikkie but in some places he has gone a little too far and over the top. But I would support him. To Frikkie I would be against in some places but also feel a little sympathetic because Tengo is blaming him for everything. I don't support Frikkie even though I feel sympathetic towards him. I even feel anger towards Frikkie because of his stupidity, but I don't feel hate towards him though.'

Alison appeared to resolve her conflicting emotions through finally making a distinction between feeling sympathetic towards Frikkie but not supporting his position and ideas. Furthermore her sympathy for him did not preclude anger 'because of his stupidity'. Out of all the students Alison seemed to come the closest to expressing a realisation of the tragedy for both Frikkie and Tengo of living under a racist system.

Final reflections

In their final reflections on the book many students wrote positively about what they felt they had learnt. For instance Julia wrote: 'The book has made me understand racism much more and I know now more about the trouble racism can cause.' On the other hand, Jacky, while writing that 'The book made me think quite a bit the world today' added 'But I expect I will soon forget. Now I think coloured people are treated much better than they were.' There appeared an element of slight defensiveness in her last sentence, written perhaps as some kind of justification for the casually honest admission 'I expect I will soon forget.'

The only student to express an extremely negative reaction to the book was Ian. It was apparent from his review that his response was deeply rooted within his increasing resistance to exploring anything to do with racism:

> 'I found the book boring because every book we have read this year is either against or for some race or colour. After a while the books started getting boring. I wish that half way through we could of had a light book not factual... I would of preferred to have done a USUAL ENGLISH year instead of research.'

Ian's conception of 'USUAL ENGLISH' requires further examination and I shall return to this in Chapter Eight. It would appear that he was appealing to the teacher's underlying view, which became increasingly apparent over the year, that exploring issues of racism and challenging racist perceptions was not really 'English'. Ian's simplistic perception that *Waiting for the Rain* was a book in favour of Tengo and against Frikkie contrasted sharply with the complexity of Alison's response. As in *Roll of Thunder, Hear My Cry* there was evidence here of racist frames of reference distorting perceptions in the transaction between writer and reader.

While there was also evidence of shifting frames of reference and examples of reperception through responding to and reflecting on texts, this did not take quite the dramatic form suggested by Dan's view that *Waiting for the Rain* would actually cause people to 'change sides':

> 'This book has given me a greater look into the problem of South Africa and also racism. I'm glad we read this book because some people who read this book, who've always been on the white's side would change sides and help the blacks because the whites stole their land and the blacks were there first. If I had the chance I'd go to South Africa and I'd try and become part of the Government and have

equality between blacks and whites. I'm surprised that the Government hasn't done anything.'

Whatever the naivete and limitations of Dan's conceptions (for example, about the nature of 'the Government' and his own ability to affect it), possibly he felt that he himself had undergone some change. However his statement has none of the personal force suggested by that of Louise:

'It made me feel angry and embaressed to admit to myself that my South African cousins are like that. They hate black people and don't have anything to do with them, they cross the road so that they don't have to walk past or look at a black person. It's disgusting the way black people are treated, after all, it is their country and white people took over the country and we treated them as heroes, as great explorers, when really they were invaders.'

Louise's statement is significantly different from Dan's in the degree to which she acknowledges involvement. Having South African cousins seemed to have helped her make the connection. She did not simply write about white people taking over the country as a distant fact, but acknowledged that 'we treated them as heroes'. Reading *Waiting for the Rain* had made her 'admit' to herself attitudes within her own family. It appeared to have engaged her in a dialogue with herself which is surely an integral part of personal change.

Chapter Seven

Approaches through drama — 'Answers that you never thought of'

The weekly drama lessons, for alternating halves of the class, were linked to the course throughout the year, with the intention that the students explore issues of justice in a range of personal and social contexts. In addition to these lessons with their English teacher Alan Parsons, there were workshops with three visiting artists, as well as with another drama teacher from the school. The students were thus briefly introduced to a variety of approaches to drama, although the focus of this chapter will be considerably narrower.

Connections with the central texts were frequently indirect and it was hoped that the students would begin to make links for themselves. While I specifically wanted the students to work with black artists, the situations of injustice which they explored did not solely relate to black/white issues. Richard Finch focused on the themes of 'the outsider' and 'survival' in relation to *Friedrich*. Millie Murray took on the roles of black characters from *Buddy* and *Roll of Thunder, Hear My Cry* and was 'hotseated' — interviewed in role — by the students. Finally, as shall be seen in the next chapter, Olusola Oyeleye led the students in a week of afternoon workshops aimed at moving from fiction to reality and encouraging the students to consider what racism might mean to them.

Assessing 'internal action'

The term 'drama' covers a wide and complex range of activities. Assessment is particularly difficult in educational drama when aiming to achieve what Bolton (1979) calls 'drama for understanding'. The primary concern here is

103

with 'internal action' in participants, namely shifts in the way they are thinking and feeling, as opposed to the directly observable 'external action'. Drama teachers aiming for shifts in 'internal action' often rely heavily on personal intuition to assess the success of a piece of drama. They might, for instance, only be able to report on a particular moment of tension at a critical, challenging point and the quality of attention which seemed to be emanating from the students. In terms of gathering the students' own commentaries, unlike in literature where the words evoking response at least remain on the page for review, in drama the stimulus is temporary and evanescent. While keeping a drama journal or diary is a valuable exercise for students to encourage reflection, it is difficult to record with accuracy finer and more detailed responses to an experience which is already receding into the past.

Occasionally some students did refer to drama sessions and while many of these comments tended to be of a general and fairly superficial nature (e.g. enjoying 'acting out' an experience), a few suggested a deeper impact. Angela and Tanya, for instance, not only made links between issues being raised in drama and those in the literature — but linked these to real life. In a dialogue between Angela and Tanya relating to *Friedrich,* tape-recorded at home (already quoted in part in Chapter Four, p.65/67), Angela can be seen moving from the principle of 'you should stick up for other people' to wondering what she would have done 'if it was back then' and her friend Tanya had been Jewish.

Tanya then connected this to a previous drama role play about some school students ostracising a religious sect, called the Jezreels but nicknamed 'Scavvies'. In the exercise Angela had been assigned the role of a 'middle-roader' (as opposed to being part of either the 'intolerant' or 'tolerant' group) but, interestingly, had moved from the neutral role into joining the taunting of the 'Scavvies'. Questioned afterwards (by the teacher) during a hotseating session, she had explained her behaviour in terms of self-protection. By taking part in the persecution she had stopped the bullies from picking on her. My impression was that Angela was somewhat embarrassed by this admission, even though she had supposedly been 'in role'. It seems quite possible that she had learnt something about herself and potential human behaviour from that role play exercise and subsequent hotseating. Perhaps this learning also contributed to her subsequently imagining herself 'back then' at the time of *Friedrich,* and to her questioning whether she would have had the strength to remain true to her principles of loyalty and equality, had her friend Tanya been Jewish.

The same taped discussion also revealed Angela and Tanya attempting to make sense of the statement that 'it is our responsibility to resist the first signs of injustice and violence'. They began by thinking of hypothetical examples in a local context, which Tanya suddenly connected to another drama lesson:

TANYA: What like um.. if you are a black.. a little black person in a cla.. in maybe a classroom um.. and and this other little kid goes.. goes 'oh look at that nigger!' and that.. and you you.. and you don't stick up for them, you are just as bad a person as the person who is saying that.

ANGELA: Yeah you should feel just as guilty (TANYA: yeah).. it's like taking um.. all the Palestinians all the Hindus all the Chinese or (TANYA: mmm) or just because of the colour or the religion or something and stationing them all in a ghetto down the road or something (TANYA: yeah yeah) and putting a ten-foot fence all the way around the town so nobody can get in.

TANYA: Oh that's like the um (ANGELA: concentration camp).. Yeah remember that drama lesson we did on that?

ANGELA: Oh yeah..

TANYA: With that um..

ANGELA: Richard Finch came in..

TANYA: That's it that's it and we all did that thing where we went into these groups and he told.. you told the uh... all your group what was the sort of incident and we did a still picture.

ANGELA: Yeah I thought that was.. I didn't like the way he was putting us in groups. I felt really like.. well I didn't feel.. I felt like a part of a class before we were put in our groups (TANYA: mmm) but after you were put in your group you felt like a part of that group (TANYA: yeah) like you were stuck to them and separated from your best friends just cause like your best friend didn't have earrings in and you did.. you were better than them. (TANYA: yeah yeah) What was your story like.. the one you told?

The lesson to which the girls were referring was Richard Finch's session on the themes of difference and being an outsider. Having begun with everyone in a large circle, including himself, sharing a piece of personal information about themselves, Richard had then begun grouping the students according to different criteria (e.g. whether they had a watch on their left hand, wore an earring, etc.) After briefly writing down what they thought made them different from anyone else, the students were put into groups and asked first to think quietly, and then tell each other, about a time when they had been made to feel an outsider. Each group had then chosen one situation out of which to create a still picture depicting exclusion.

What seemed significant in Angela and Tanya's discussion is the way in which they connected the affective personal experience within drama to their cognitive understanding of wider social issues. While Angela was far more articulate and dominant than Tanya, in the privacy of this conversation between friends, Tanya (who only spoke out in class if specifically called upon by the teacher) was not only an active listener, but actually made the links with their previous drama lessons, perceiving their relevance.

Hotseating

Given the difficulties of assessment in educational drama, I intend to focus the major part of this chapter on those sessions most closely connected to the literature — those involving 'hotseating' characters from the novels. Apart from both questions and replies often being revealing about the perceptual frames of the participants, the texts also provide a fixed point of reference for readers to consider students' interpretations.

Hotseating was a feature of the course which received unanimous approval from the students in their final evaluations of the course. It is a drama technique which can be useful in a variety of contexts and for a variety of purposes. For instance, it can be used within a drama session to deepen the level of understanding within dramatic playing, by breaking off to interview one of the players in role with the intention of taking the drama deeper and further. It can equally be used within a classroom setting during the reading of a novel, by stopping to interview some of the characters in role, in order to gain clarification about the inter-relationships. From a teacher's point of view, it can also reveal gaps in students' understandings of the text. One element of hotseating which might be thought problematic is that there is immediate imbalance with only the interviewee in role. Nevertheless, although it is possible for both parties to remain involved at only an intellectual level in the exercise, it is also possible that the person being hotseated moves deeper into the role and the feelings of 'as if'. This in turn might deepen the other participants' sense of actually getting to 'know' the character being role-played, affectively as well as cognitively.

It was with this possibility in mind, and with the specific purpose of using hotseating as a means of challenging students' perceptions, that the writer Millie Murray was invited to work with the students in relation to the novels *Buddy* and *Roll of Thunder, Hear My Cry*. Her brief was to be interviewed in role as various black characters in the novels and through her responses to challenge any possible misconceptions. Indeed it was hoped that she might be able to disturb some of the mental and emotional underpinning for complacency about racism. Millie's perspective very much reflected that of Mildred Taylor who herself acknowledged concern with reframing perceptions and showing 'a different kind of Black world' — through a black family surviving the onslaught of a discriminatory society with strength and dignity (English Centre 1984).

Students' perceptions of black characters from *Buddy*

Aspirations such as these were central to the idea of Millie Murray being invited to work with the students. The idea germinated after I had observed a hotseating session amongst the students relating to characters in *Buddy*. Hotseated as the white working-class Buddy, Ian's racist perceptions revealed themselves in the way he justified Buddy's friendship with the black Rybeero twins:

> PAUL: Once you said some nasty things about black kids so what why are you changed now?
>
> IAN: Because they sort of show me that they're not really black. They're sort of the same as me.

Ian's response to the twins was clearly assimilationist. Did any other students perhaps also hold 'whitened' images of them? Further evidence of an essentially negative, albeit unwitting, perception relating to black people came from an unexpected source, namely Angela. Hotseated as Charmian, Angela role-played her as passively putting up with racism, rather than reacting with any anger:

> DONALD: What do you think about all the other kids in your class, how they treat you?
>
> ANGELA: Oh I just shrug it off. You get used to it after a while. I mean quite a lot of kids are racist I suppose. I mean I've got my brother.. my twin to stick with so I don't really mind....
>
> TERRY: If Buddy asked you out what would you say?
>
> ANGELA: I'd probably say yes, but he'd probably get a lot of stick from all the other white kids so if it was for his sake I'd say no.

Asked about her parents, she spoke of them being supportive and 'jolly', cheering her up when necessary, but admitted to feeling shame at times:

> A.P: Are you sometimes embarrassed by them (your parents) in the way Buddy is sometimes embarrassed by his father?
>
> ANGELA: I don't think in the same way. I mean I don't mind their taste in things. Sometimes I get ashamed of my colour and their colour.
>
> A.P: Why?
>
> ANGELA: Because although people say that my mother is really jolly and she reflects on people and makes them happy and things, sometimes when we are walking together people give her funny looks and things.

Given that Angela was the most outspoken, self-confident girl in the class, articulating strong views on equality, it seemed of note that she had not imagined that Charmian would reject insults more forcefully. Angela's interpretation of Charmian also seemed in marked contrast to her stated pride in her own Irish origins. Despite her Southern British Standard English accent, she had declared boldly in the first survey: 'I think about how lucky I am to be Irish and I am never ashamed.' Nor was her interpretation grounded in the text. Charmian is not present when the racist joking takes place and we do not hear any commentary from her on it. Whenever we see her, she is confident, caring and perceptive. The ways that Angela filled the gaps in the text (Iser 1978) and the sort of predictions she made, suggested the possibility of significant cultural stereotyping which needed to be challenged.

Further drama work focused on status and power, the students being directly asked to fill a gap in the text by improvising the scene on Parents' Evening between the racist teacher Mr Normington and the Rybeeros. Angela, playing Mrs Rybeero, hotly defended her son but did not raise the issue of racism. However, in the following week's improvisation, the astute Philip, playing Mr Rybeero, openly confronted Mr Normington, played by the teacher Alan Parsons:

> PHILIP: Can you explain why you complain when Charmian is being quiet and you complain when her brother is the opposite? Would you prefer them both to be dumb?

> A.P: No Mr Rybeero. What I am asking is for Julian to think before he speaks and Carmian (sic) to speak at all. I would appreciate it if you would say something to them about this. (A.P. deliberately mispronouncing the twins' names)

> PHILIP: I just think Charmian is intimidated by whites. If you go into any High Street white people will take the micky out of her.

The meeting ended however with 'Mr Normington' slickly defusing the conflict, with general agreement from the students that this role play seemed realistic. Sympathy clearly rested with the Rybeeros who had been out-manipulated, but they nevertheless remained framed in terms of 'intimidated victims'.

Other signs that common stereotypes and fears amongst some members of the class could be tapped without much difficulty also emerged in the class discussion about Buddy's experience at the Satellite Youth Club, most of whose members were black, and with the black boy Dennis in particular (Chapter Three, p.47/50). These included Ian's view of Dennis as 'sort of a typical black because they sort of judge you', Graham's description of the Youth Club as a 'very very strange environment' and John's statement about being 'frightened' and feeling 'out of place and all these black people looking at you and people staring'.

Millie Murray as Charmian and Mrs Rybeero

Once Millie Murray had agreed to be hotseated — first as Charmian, speaking Standard English, and then as her mother, Mrs Rybeero, speaking Jamaican English — the students were asked if they would like to meet the two of them, ten years on from the book. Initial scepticism about a 'real' Charmian soon turned to enthusiasm. The class wrote their expectations of what Charmian might now be like and potential questions for the visitors. Millie was sent these, with a copy of the students' own hotseating session, giving her an idea of the implicit stereotypes she would be attempting to counter.

Initially almost all the students were taken in by Millie's Charmian. She was presented as a resourceful, articulate writer who, reflecting Millie's own career, had previously been a psychiatric nurse and a secretary. Suspicions were only aroused when she re-appeared as a motherly, outspoken Mrs Rybeero, whose sharp tongue reduced Mr Normington to 'that wicked, evil man!' This part of the session was peppered with laughter, largely at Millie's versatile parrying of questions aimed at detecting her true identity. Through both characters, however, Millie introduced a range of challenging attitudes.

Asked about the racist jokes in the 'Express' class, Millie's Charmian combined perceptive sympathy for Buddy's desire not to be an outcast, with contempt for the initiators of the racism who

> 'didn't openly come out.. and that gave me strength. I felt good about that.. because that's what bullies are like you know people who are racist who have these racist attitudes.. making snide remarks.. they could never come up and say 'you jungle-bunny'.. as you walk by you catch it but you're walking by...'

Reflecting on Mr Normington's 'man-made air of self-importance', she made it clear that although Charmian had not been able to confront him as a child, this did not imply getting 'used to' the abuse:

> '..the snide remarks he used to make about my colour I um found very offensive.. but you know.. it's not something.. really that.. you can um dwell on too much.. because I think it could make you quite violent actually.. you know if someone never liked you because of your colour or... you spoke differently or... you come from a place that's different from them or your eyes are blue or your religion is different... so now on reflection when I think of Mr Normington.. I do feel angry at times when I think of all the times when I really could have stood up to him but.. I pity him.. because he obviously has a problem.... to be that way to young people. I wonder if he would be that way perhaps.. to a black man.. you know on an equal level to him.. perhaps not.'

In Millie's characterisation of Charmian it can be seen that Mr Normington's abuse of power had not ultimately won the day — either by provoking her to 'dwell on' it too much in sheer anger, or by her accepting the demeaning message. Indeed the provocation seemed to have encouraged Millie's Charmian to become more resilient. She was able to see Mr Normington in terms of a wider human canvas. By relating his racism to other kinds of discrimination and particularly to his domination of young people, Millie opened out a number of links for her audience to consider.

Responding to questions on a range of issues, Millie's Charmian and Mrs Rybeero were not one-dimensional 'victims', but individuals contending with — and resisting — racism as part of full, active lives. The nature of the session in which the students hotseated Millie differed in a fundamental respect from the previous session in which they had interviewed other members of the class in role. Even when it was clear that Millie was not actually Charmian but was playing a role — in other words that she was in the 'as if' mode — she was obviously bringing to the role her own experience as a black woman, thus increasing the dimension of reality.

Coming out of role, Millie initiated small group drama work. Given a fictional entry in Charmian's diary about Mr Normington endorsing yet more racist baiting, the students were asked to improvise a subsequent scene with Charmian and friends. It was a task they found difficult, Millie intervening at one point to ask them how they would feel if the discrimination was against their religion. In a short debriefing, the teacher commented on how they conveyed a sense of powerlessness in dealing with the harassment.

The session concluded with a version of Forum Theatre with Millie as Charmian, aged twenty-four, unexpectedly meeting Mr Normington, played by Philip. Other students, sitting in a circle around the two main protagonists, volunteered to be various characters from the book. As the confrontation developed, Charmian and Mr Normington each called on people to speak in their defence. Philip (who as Mr Rybeero had made an able attempt to stand up to Alan Parsons' Mr Normington) quickly found himself overpowered by Charmian's direct accusations with her open, dogged insistence that Mr Normington had allowed racism to go unchallenged in his classroom. The discussion became increasingly heated, with Donald suddenly accusing Charmian of fabricating evidence because she had a 'chip on her shoulder'. Her reply was straightforward:

> 'My memory is very good and I haven't got a problem. You see the reason you told me I've got a problem you see is because you're not black.'

Unfortunately further developments were cut short by the bell.

Discussions the following day in groups and with the whole class were revealing. Assumptions about black women held by Ian and John — concerning fertility and achievement — had certainly been challenged although there was no indication they would be altered. Indeed two-thirds of the class had predicted Charmian would be married and almost half that she would have children:

> TANYA: I thought Charmian would be.. would have a family by now.

> IAN: I think it's really um.. that you think of her from a Jamaican I think.. you see um.. quite a lot of black children around so I thought she would have started a family up already.'

Tanya's response can probably be interpreted in the light of a focus on women as mothers, or her own love of children (wanting to work with them), although in an interview she didn't see herself starting a family, saying 'It's too much responsibility'.

Ian, however, openly admitted to having thought of Charmian 'from a Jamaican' [point of view]. Later, apparently egged on by Ian, John acknowledged his surprise at Millie being a writer. The giggles and intonation of the exchange suggest an awareness amongst the group of the racist connotations:

> IAN: I think John wants to say something now!

> JOHN: (brief giggle) I was surprised when um the school got an author.. I thought they would have just got a black woman off the streets.. you know someone they knew or something. (controlling giggle)

> ANGELA: Oh no! (laughter)

> IAN: That's not very nice! (loud, possibly to convey affected shock)

> JOHN: No! Not off the streets! But someone the school knew (giggle) or somebody like that! (controls laugh)

> NEIL: No I don't thinks so John.. I mean-

> JOHN: I was surprised when they got an author though.

> NEIL: It's supposed to be pretty organised! They wouldn't just sort of go out and say 'Would you like to come and do that?'

In contrast, Marco affirmed in another group how much he had enjoyed supporting Charmian in her exchange with Mr Normington. While refraining from speaking of his own experiences since arriving in England from Italy three years previously, Marco commented: 'I suppose you get the same kind of situation if somebody was Irish.' However, some months later and in private, he spoke of his personal shock at having been 'put down' as an Italian by a particular teacher.

A number of students acknowledged that the experience with Millie had brought new realisations to them about the hurt caused by racist name-calling, although Philip's tone possibly suggested a slightly ambivalent response to what he perceived as 'a moral message':

> PHILIP: I thought it was good cause um.. we didn't really understand how blacks feel when they are called racist things.. and we had to try and understand.. (slowing down speech for last phrase — affected?)

> DAN: I think we understood how black people cope.. when they.. when um people make racist remarks at them.. and I think we just.. we just think we know what they do.. when they get back.. but.. they really feel.. hurt.

> MARION: But we will never know how they really feel because we are not black ourselves so we will never get the racist remarks that they get.. so.. we won't know exactly.

> CAROLINE: Yeah but we had a good practice when we were doing the um.. the acting out.. it was pretty good.. we learnt a lot.

Marion's remark was the most perceptive, suggesting a deep affective level of knowledge derived from experience and not fully penetrable by cognitive understanding alone. Caroline, however, identified the value of drama as a means of learning about the experience of others. Sentiments similar to those of the two boys, suggesting they had not previously understood the degree of hurt, were also expressed by others:

> SIMON: I still think that er.. I didn't realise how much the um black people felt offended by it....

However Simon was unable to share Michelle's acknowledgement that she now had a better understanding of Dennis' hostile response to Buddy:

> MICHELLE: ....now I realise that he'd been having.. you know he's been having all this trouble from you know the white kids at school.... and so now I realise.... why he was so off to um Buddy.

> SIMON: I understand how Dennis feels but I don't know why he took it out on Buddy....

> ANDREW: But at least there's not.. not very much racialism in this school. ('I'm saying the right thing' tone?)

It is difficult to pin-point undercurrents of tone, but nonetheless I thought it worth recording where the way a statement was spoken suggested it might have been made simply for public consumption. Andrew, having lived in South Africa for a number of years, was likely to be more aware than most of the challenge Millie presented to racist ideas. Certainly there was the potential for him to feel more uncomfortable than most. Apart from a couple of occasions in small group discussion where he had ended up more or less defending apartheid and his family's right to have a black servant at the bottom of their garden, I had the feeling he generally kept such challenges at bay by consciously saying the 'right' thing. In the class discussion that followed group talk on Millie's session, Alan Parsons homed in on Andrew:

A.P: Did it do anything to your um attitudes?

ANDREW: Yes.

A.P: What?

ANDREW: Um.. what do you mean by um you know...

A.P: Have you ever been in a position where you've had um a black person speaking to you in that way before?

ANDREW: N-n-

A.P: ...addressing you in that way before?

ANDREW: N-no. Not as I can recall, no.

A.P: Did it surprise you? (Andrew nods) What?

ANDREW: Um how straightforward she was and you know started to talk just talked about it like um normally like a normal person.

Here Andrew unwittingly revealed that black people for him usually came into a category other than normal. It is impossible to know what lasting effect Millie Murray's visit might have had on his frames of reference. He may possibly have moved to a position of conceding some black people to be 'normal', while still maintaining that the 'garden-boy' in South Africa was happy working for his family and living in a room at the bottom of their garden.

A number of students made the point that Millie had expected a lot of them. While there is no evidence that they would have commented differently had Millie been white, I hoped this had challenged black 'deficit' imagery. Many students asked whether Millie might return and generally there was considerable appreciation of the experience she had created, as expressed here by Gaby and Julia:

GABY: I thought it was good of her to talk about her race and everything 'cause it sort of broke the barrier down.

Journal entry by Julia:
'The work we had to do was good fun and it realised to me how much whites are racist before then I never bothered. Charmian answered all questions well and I thought she had a good ambition.'

Roll of Thunder, Hear My Cry and the power divide

The opportunity for Millie to return arose a few months later, with *Roll of Thunder, Hear My Cry*. Once again, discussion and hotseating amongst the students themselves revealed some significant misconceptions. In particular I was concerned that the Logan children were being regarded as harsh for not accepting the white boy Jeremy's offers of friendship. A common view seemed to be 'If he is loyal to them, why aren't they loyal to him?' Making judgements from within the confines of their own experience, they seemed to have little idea of the enormous power divide between white and black in America of the 1930s.

In preparation for Millie's second session — and to give her an idea of their perceptions — the students were asked to draft film scripts developing a dialogue between Cassie and Jeremy after Cassie suspects his family of involvement in burning a neighbour's house. Only a few of these scripts, however, depicted the confrontation with any real tension, although many of the scripts reveal Jeremy taking a 'just let's be friends' line.

Millie Murray as Cassie, Mama and Big Ma: the challenge of a black perspective

For this session it was clear to the students from the start that Millie would be role-playing. Beginning as Cassie, then with her hair up as Mama, Cassie's mother, and finally putting on a headscarf and becoming Big Ma, the grandmother, Millie took the students through the three generations of Logan women. Apart from changing her hairstyle, Millie reflected the changes in personae in intonation and manner of speaking, as well as in the perspective she conveyed for each character.

Whereas less than a quarter of the questions directed to Millie on the previous occasion as Charmian and Mrs Rybeero were connected to issues of racism, nearly 85 per cent of Millie's answers as Cassie, Mama and Big Ma related to racism and, in particular, the psychological responses derived from living under racist oppression. For instance, replying to a question from Philip about why she had been 'so nice' to Jeremy's sister Lillian Jean after the latter had humiliated her, Millie gave an explanation beyond the mere fact that Cassie was planning to get her own back:

> MILLIE: I was just you know thinking that if I just play up to her.. you know like a sweet little 'nigger' girl.. she wouldn't really know what was in my mind.. and she never! That's how stupid people are! You know when people think they have power over you.. they just think that you are stupid... just because they're poor and sometimes cause we're black.. we're not stupid you know... Let me ask you all a question.. what would you do in my situation? How would you feel in my situation? (pause) Well you ain't got no tongue.. you can't talk? Cause you can't imagine what it's like to be in my situation.. cause

when you're born black you stay black till you die.. and you know being black is not a problem. It's just a problem to white people.. to some white people...'

Many of the students' questions about how Cassie felt about certain characters provided Millie with an opportunity to open out deeper social as well as psychological dynamics. For instance when she was asked 'Do you really hate Mr Simms?' (Jeremy's father), she attempted to clarify that her angry feelings — indeed hatred — should be distinguished from 'race' hate:

GIRL (unidentified voice): Do you really hate Mr. Simms?

MILLIE: Well.. I guess I do.. I mean I don't just hate him cause he's a white man and he's Lillian Jean's papa.. I hate him because he's not a nice man.. you know well he probably just hate me cause I'm black.

A number of questions were put to Millie, both as Cassie and Mama, concerning their feelings about Jeremy. As Cassie, Millie attempted to explain that although she could recognise Jeremy's positive qualities, the situation in which they lived could not be ignored.

MARION: What did you think of the present Jeremy gave to Stacey.. the flute?

MILLIE: Well I don't know.. it was a nice gesture I suppose you know. I mean Jeremy does try but.. well it's kinda like a difficult situation cause unless you live in that kind of oppression.. you may not understand what.. what's happening down there you know.

A little later Philip asked how she would feel if Jeremy died, presumably trying to test her feelings about Jeremy further, and Tanya wanted to know how she compared Jeremy with T.J., who although black was untrustworthy. After an intervening question on how she compared the situation of Jewish people with that of black people, Millie was once again brought back to Jeremy and the uneasy question of trusting white people:

MICHELLE: How would you feel if Jeremy turned against you and then didn't want to go around with you?

MILLIE: Well to tell the truth it wouldn't surprise me none.. you know because where I come from you just don't trust white folk.. you just don't trust them at all.. no matter how friendly and how loving and how nice they can be to y'all...

While Millie, both as Mama and Big Ma, came across as more restrained and calm in her responses, the underlying message about it not being safe to trust white people nevertheless remained the same.

Following the hotseating, Millie created a short improvisation with herself as Cassie and Peter volunteering to play Jeremy. Using the same starting point as the film script, Millie as Cassie confronted Peter as Jeremy with news of a house being burnt in the night by white people. Peter's first response was to defend his father, saying he would not have been involved. However after persistent challenges from Millie, he changed to saying that he had not the power to stop his father. Cassie should accept that he himself felt differently and they should not let this spoil their friendship. Millie in role as Cassie, however, refused to let him off the hook, forcing him to admit that if his father insisted, he would accompany him on a burning expedition. The scene ended with Cassie expressing disgust. How could they be friends on that basis?

While there had been some laughter from the students at a couple of points where Peter was working himself into the accent and dialect of Jeremy, it appeared that his active involvement with Millie in the role play had directly challenged and affected him. In the writing workshop that followed, Peter diverged from the task set the class by Millie. Instead he produced a piece of writing in role as Jeremy which was impressive not only for its authentic tone of voice ('My Papa sure scares me 'bout the other night') but as a statement about how he would make a stand against his father. Usually fairly reticent, Peter volunteered to read this to the class. It seemed he had become involved in more than an exercise.

Although journal entries revealed that students had enjoyed this session, there was a feeling that the *Buddy* event had been more fun. Certainly the majority of questions to Millie on *Roll of Thunder, Hear My Cry* led into serious issues, in which racism had shifted centre-stage. In addition Millie's perspective was one which challenged the notion that racism is simply a matter of personal feelings and that as long as a white person does not feel personally hostile towards black people, then she or he can be dissociated from anti-black racism in the society.

Reflection: possibilities and limitations

In articulating the value of drama, Simon wrote in his journal:

> 'I find that when drama is being carried out, I usually understand what is happening better.'

Certainly the evidence of Peter's response following his role play with Millie suggests the possible power of drama, although clearly a significant factor in that particular interchange was the weight of reality which Millie carried as Cassie.

It would seem that for students to move into the realm of Bolton's 'drama for understanding' (1979) it is necessary for them to have both structure and a challenging focus as well as the space to feel their own sense of control over, and responsibility for, the drama. A teacher who can move in and out of role her or himself — at times to further the internal drama or to halt it for external reflection — may be in the best position to enable students to face up to difficult challenges at an emotional as well as intellectual level. What is possibly critical is that the teacher be seen to be equally investing in the drama — and the drama only works because there is an agreement to trust each other. The drama is thus removed from a realm in which a teacher simply sets up activities and relies on her or his authority for students to perform. There are fundamental issues here related to the kinds of pedagogical frameworks which need to be developed for undertaking work in exploring racism with students, to which I shall return in my final chapter.

While hotseating was not generally embedded within drama in this way, it nevertheless appeared to have been of value in terms of the specific purposes for which it was used in the project, namely eliciting students' perceptions and offering challenges to some of those perceptions through the hotseating of Millie Murray. Comments made by some of the students in a discussion, led by Alan Parsons immediately after Millie's second session, indicated some of the strengths of hotseating:

'You sort of get right down deep in yourself and pull out all the answers.' (John)

'It makes you ask things that you don't really understand.' (Greg)

'When people who are hotseated are asked questions they seem to have answers that you never thought of.' (Philip)

While, as in drama generally, it is not possible to measure how stereotypes may or may not have shifted towards perceptions of a fuller reality, these responses suggest the potential of hotseating to be personal, active and exploratory for both interviewer and interviewee. However, it is necessary also to recognise its limits and that sensitive debriefing is essential. For instance, in hotseating characters from a text, basic misunderstandings or misreadings may be revealed. Furthermore a character portrayed through hotseating is itself a construction, derived not only from the text but from the life experiences of the person in the chair. It would have been valuable, for instance, for the students to have spent time after Millie's sessions actually contrasting their previous responses with hers, in order to draw out the links between her portrayals and her own experience as a black person in a white dominated society.

Given that the interpretation or construction of black characters by white students would be limited by their own frames of reference, a major question arises about how to challenge limitations in perception when there is no recourse to someone like Millie Murray. There are a number of possible strategies. A teacher who was aware of the issues could offer to be hotseated alongside students in order to present a more critical black perspective or, given sufficient confidence, might use teacher-in-role within drama. First-hand testimonies of black people can very effectively be used to develop the drama (see Dodgson 1984).

Students might also increase their understanding by exploring other situations of oppression but in more familiar contexts. The latter approach provides the rationale for John Twitchin's 'Target Group' exercise (1988) and underlies much current work on human rights education as well as the developing theory and practice of anti-racist education in predominantly white primary schools (Epstein and Sealey 1990; Brown, Barnfield and Stone 1990). It is also important to have access to a range of related materials to raise awareness. For instance, poetry and music might be able to convey to some students the 'voice' they may have been missing and open the door for some students to experience the celebratory sense of resistance of people who have not allowed themselves to become dehumanised by racism.

Whatever the ways in which one might attempt to open up such doors, however, Millie Murray posed a final question at the end of her second workshop which indicates a continuing challenge:

'You know, unless you are sort of living under oppression of any kind, can you fully understand it?'

Chapter Eight

From fiction to reality — responses to a direct focus on racism

The need to bring issues home

My original intention was for the students to return at the end of the course to literature focusing on racism in a British context. However, as study of the preceding novels took longer than I had predicted, I decided to broaden my original remit of using responses to fiction as the primary route in to the exploration of racism. The students' responses to the subsequent change of medium involving a direct focus on racism, and the manner in which the course began to be reperceived by a number of students, raised important issues which had not previously surfaced.

The television programmes

While the students were still reading *Waiting for the Rain*, I arranged for them to view the BBC series *Getting to Grips with Racism* (BBC 1988) with a Senior Teacher, Gerald Carey, during Religious Education periods in the summer term. If they had not already deduced it, it must have been clear at this point to the students that my interest in their responses extended beyond the broad domain of literature and related particularly to questions of racism.

The tone of the series itself is very direct, the producer Peter Evans writing in the Teacher's Guide that they had decided not to approach their subject in a nervous manner:

> Racism will not go away if we creep up on it and circle round it. Only if the audience is left in no doubt about its nature, will they be able to go on to do something about it.

The first programme explains what is meant by racism and looks at the kinds of racism young people may experience and raises issues of the role of schools and anti-racist policies. Programme two looks at racism in the local community — for instance graffiti, racist attacks, relations with the police and discrimination in employment — and how black people have been trying to deal with these questions. The third programme moves on to the wider area of national and institutional racism, examining the role of the media and the effect of government policies, especially in the field of immigration. Finally programme four returns to the classroom, looking at the hidden messages in the curriculum and resources, raising questions of what is taught and what is omitted.

Ideally the series should be shown over an eight to ten week period, with sufficient time for the students to become actively involved with the issues of each unit before moving on to the next. The project students had approximately half this space, with no allocation of homework time to develop initiatives beyond the classroom. In retrospect it would have been wiser to have selected only a couple of the programmes, developing more activities around them, rather than attempting to cover all four.

Making issues and attitudes explicit

The most notable feature of the shift in medium was the way in which putting racism 'up front' — and virtually on the doorstep — began to elicit openly negative reactions from those students who in the survey had shown themselves most willing to identify themselves with explicitly racist statements, albeit anonymously. In their responses to fiction, racism was more often implicit than a matter of explicit statement. In addition, an element of defensiveness also began to appear in a number of students.

Before looking at the negative reactions in more detail, I want to focus briefly on some of the strongly positive responses against racism which the programmes elicited as well. Many of the students for instance indicated shock at racist behaviour on the part of the police, while some students appeared taken aback at the way black MPs have to protect themselves and their families against physical attacks. Writing immediately after the film on immigration, more than half the students expressed strongly affective responses, such as:

> 'The programme made me realise how terrible racism is.' (Paul)

> 'I was appauled that the government split families up until they have proved that someone one is related to another...' (Neil)

'I thought how discusting it was for the two black boys to be sent away and be split up of their family.' (Peter)

The programmes appeared to serve a genuinely informative function for some students about examples of racism and injustice in our society. While this was very important, one has to remember that these were students who tended to openness in the first place and that simply evoking strong affective responses against racism would not in itself equip them to argue more effectively against racist thinking.

The films did attempt to encourage students to think about connections between racism and power. However the definition of racism offered to the viewers was the simplified, personalised one of 'prejudice + power':

'It's being prejudiced against people from different backgrounds and cultures and taking some kind of action to do them down, to injure them and to humiliate them.' (Terry Badoo, Programme Presenter)

Even before the film, more than two-thirds of the students' own definitions of racism included some notion of action, with about a third also implicitly containing the idea of one group being more powerful. However at the same time the students tended to see the primary source of the conflict, or 'putting down', residing rather simply in people's personal or group dislikes — indeed sometimes hatred — of those of another 'race', colour or culture. Examining the roots of prejudice and racism in human behaviour is a complex task involving the study of our history and how we have been shaped by economic, political, social as well as psychological factors (Hall 1981). In order to begin developing a more complex understanding of racism and power — including the idea of prejudices as rationalisations which help to perpetuate oppression based on 'race' — the students may well have benefited from engaging in active learning situations, such as simulations or games, very specifically devised to explore the relationship of racism, power and prejudice. They needed to confront racist arguments for themselves and to begin to understand their social origin and function in society. As it was, the programmes tended to reinforce the focus on personal/group hostility and racism at a surface level, with quite a number of students acknowledging surprise at the degree of hatred and viciousness behind racist attacks.

Negative reactions to the programme quickly came to the fore. Despite a written declaration that he was 'totally against racism', Terry stated in discussion after the first programme that 'They can think what they like. It's up to them.. the whites.. if they like blacks that's O K, if they don't that's up to them.' Gerald Carey asked the class for responses to Terry's view:

G.C.: How many people agree with what Terry is saying? You're entitled to be a racist is what Terry is saying.. if you want to be.... Should we, in fact, influence people not to be racist? Or should we take Terry's view... if you want to be a racist.. if you want to call people 'Nigger',

'Paki', 'Paddy', 'Mick', then that is entirely up to you and you should be allowed to do that? ...Carl?

CARL: No you should perhaps try to put people off.. not influence-

G.C.: You would disagree with Terry?

CARL: No not really because-

G.C.: Oh you wouldn't disagree?

CARL: Well yeah it's still bad but.. it's like we were told that you've got free choice to do what you want.. in the Bible and that, so that if you're given free choice, you should do what you want to do.

G.C.: The Bible says very clearly... 'Love God and love your neighbour as yourself.' That is a command!...

JOHN: I feel you have a right to think whatever you like but I think you should keep it to yourself.

.....

G.C.: ...But if I feel like calling you names, isn't there something... intrinsically wrong with me... that I want to pick on someone different from me? (Bell for end of lesson)

It is clear that discussion about racism in this Religious Education context had become very direct in relation to the students' own attitudes and lives, with the teacher taking a strong moral position. His questions would have left the students in no doubt as to the kind of answers he was hoping to elicit. It is worth noting that the students engaging with the teacher — John, Terry and Carl — were three of the four students expressing the most explicit racist views on the second survey. The fourth, Ian, did not join in at all at this stage.

Carl's ambivalence is interesting, torn between being seen to agree with the teacher's moral position — and thus acknowledging disagreement with his friend Terry — and asserting his own right to free choice, wherever that might lead. As the student who showed the most marked increase in explicit racism on the second survey (from a low to medium-high level), Carl was particularly disturbing. Although the rise was very likely the result of a complex of factors — with personal factors beyond the realm of school — the anti-authority element in his response has pedagogical implications for teaching about racism.

Unlike Carl, neither John nor Ian showed any ambivalence. In commenting on racist graffiti, for instance, John noted that 'I would be offended if they said anything about my family'. John's grandparents came to England as immigrants from Poland and he was prepared to assert directly his belief in the rights of white people:

'I think the blacks, Indians came over to England they should abide by our rules. I think that whites should get the upper hand on a job.'

Predictably, he was very hostile to the programme on immigration and media representation of black people:

'I felt that they didn't show both sides to the story, they only said the points that would stand out... Then they complain about the press being byias but the riots do happen. Asian people were just trying to blame it on other people!'

Ian's written response showed him also sharply critical of what he perceived as an attack on white people:

'the T.V. programme is given a black advantage. So they are telling us that all the whites are wrong to write anything about blacks and the blacks are totally and utterley innocent.'

He seemed more concerned, however, about openly voicing his racist views to the teacher. Speaking for the first time only after the final programme, he brought up the question of golliwogs in books and his belief that as a young child he had 'read it without thinking' i.e. without being influenced. In his written notes he was much more openly negative about his resentment of the programme's perspective:

'Black people are just trying to make themselves a place in society. They have started off all the racism by making protests about non intensionally written books towards blacks.'

Ian's position here is the familiar one of projecting the source of the problem onto the victims, who are seen as the perpetrators guilty of provoking racism through their protests.

While the programmes posed challenges to students' views, there was no obvious evidence of those views undergoing any immediate change. Michael provided a very interesting example of a student who found himself challenged but then simply accommodated the contradictory perceptions. In response to the second programme on racism in the community, he wrote:

'There seems to be strong racism when blacks are trying to seek employment. The whites always get the more superior job. I don't mind there being a black M.P. but how it appeared to me, they just wanted to do this just to show the white people that they can get high jobs. When he [Paul Boateng] said 'We have waited for 400 years for this' this to me is a bit wrong because like I said they are just trying to get there own back which I suppose they have a right to do.'

Michael was confused. On the one hand he felt compelled to recognise that black people have been denied their rights, yet at the same time he seemed to be threatened by the tone of the black MP, Paul Boateng in his election victory speech. An apparently gentle and sensitive boy, his deeply embedded racist perceptions nevertheless overrode his acknowledgement of the injustice experienced by black people.

A clear example of the capacity to accommodate contradictory perceptions was revealed in his response to the programme on immigration:

> 'When they were talking about programs making racial jokes this can be quite harmful to the black people, but to us and the T.V. producers it's just a bit of harmless fun. Over the imigration laws I think that trying to prove that it's your family is a bit petty but the government has to control the amount of people coming into this country because it could become very overcrowded. With the white population growing and black population growing England can only take so much people. I thought it was terrible when that football supporter threw a banna at the black football player.'

Michael's description of British immigration law policy which results in the separation of families as 'a bit petty' contrasts strikingly, for instance, with his strong sympathy for the central character of Buddy when he was separated from his mother. In his group he had commented about Buddy: 'I mean a boy can't survive without his mother you know'. Although the programme had shown two Asian boys forced to be apart from their mother for four years because of immigration laws, Michael's construct of 'overcrowding' in Britain appeared to override any sympathetic feelings he might have had for them.

From a teaching point of view, the key issue is how to encourage students to reflect on and examine illogicalities in their thinking. Where they arise within a journal response, one possibility, if time permits, is for the teacher to engage in written dialogue with the student. Effective use might also be made of focused small group discussions, avoiding the constraints of the whole class format where the teacher might find her or himself constantly putting forward the anti-racist propositions from a position of authority. One needs to create space for those students who do experience strong responses against racism to gain confidence in articulating their views so that they might be more able to contribute to larger class discussions. Given that the girls on the whole tended towards more open non-racist responses, this has important implications for adressing gender relations in the classroom. Yet as in the class discussions in English, girls participated notably less than boys in these R.E. sessions.

A brief questionnaire on immigration was aimed at stimulating reflection before and after the third programme of *Getting to Grips with Racism*. At face value, the film and an accompanying information sheet appeared at least to correct a number of misapprehensions held by the majority of students. However one needs to be extremely cautious about interpreting this kind of cognitive-response data as evidence of real learning. While it is obviously important to ensure students have access to correct information and that misinformation is challenged, perceptions concerning issues of 'race' are deeply embedded within us at an affective level, affecting how such information is actually received (Klineberg 1950; Allport 1954). It seems likely that on completing the questionnaire for a second time, students such as Ian, John and Michael supplied the correct replies about Britain's population getting smaller, without any fundamental shifts in what they 'knew' and their own deep internal 'knowledge' concerning immigration.

Glimpses into the wider context

A few small incidents surrounding the fourth R.E. session might provide a glimpse into some aspects of the wider context which were also likely to have impinged on the students' perceptions. While preparing the video equipment in the classroom, I was asked by the head of the Religious Education department whether the students were not getting tired of 'all this' about racism. 'Shouldn't they be just enjoying books for fun?' This was followed by the students' usual R.E. teacher taking four students out of the class (before the arrival of Gerald Carey and without any consultation) to practise an assembly which he had just agreed to do. This was the second time he had done this and it clearly indicated that he saw any sessions on racism as optional. It was also during this fourth session that students began to ask me about my name. Was I really Beverley Naidoo and not Ms Trewhela and had I written *Journey to Jo'burg?* It appeared that their R.E. teacher had, without informing me, revealed my dual identity! As a result Gerald Carey and I decided that the final session should be changed to allow the students an opportunity to ask me questions about myself, instead of being wholly devoted to evaluation.

Students' evaluations

Interestingly, the immediate evaluations of the sessions were generally more positive than those made three weeks later to the external evaluator, Chris Gaine, a Senior Lecturer in Education and Racial Equality. Unfortunately half the girls were absent for the external evaluation and this no doubt affected the overall class impression. It appeared, nevertheless, that a few students later felt the programmes had been boring or always on 'the same subject'. Some of the students making negative comments surprised me — such as Alison, Peter and Paul. They had appeared positively involved at the time and I wondered whether these responses may have been in part a reaction against the over-simplistic 'prejudice + power' formulation of white racism inherent in the programmes — the focus of which was in fact largely continued during the 'Media Week' workshops. Donald's comment that the series was 'allright but it was only about black racism not about the Jews ETC' linked closely to a common response to the Media Week. Students making positive comments on the series focused largely on the programmes being informative.

The students' responses to *Getting to Grips with Racism,* both throughout the series and in later evaluation, raised a number of issues which had not arisen before in relation to the literature. Whether or not these issues would have arisen had the course ended as originally planned — exploring racism in a local British context through literature — is a matter for speculation. Television works as a different medium and the programmes were not only concerned with communicating information which related to life in Britain today, but the students clearly constituted a 'target audience'. The programmes also carried a clear moral message about the unacceptability of racism.

The students' perceptions of my own agenda, which had previously been far more loosely defined in connection with their responses to literature, albeit literature of a particular character, also probably became more closely defined — all the more so after the revelation of my dual identity. Statements made by both Angela and Donald in their final R.E. session suggested that the whole project might have been in danger of becoming reduced in their mental maps to having been 'only about racism'. This kind of redefinition and reduction of the year's literature course, which had in fact opened out a wide range of literary and related experiences to the students, appeared to become more widespread over Media Week. This response cannot be disassociated from the teacher's own disaffection which I shall shortly explore. Given vulnerable feelings being aroused in the students, they needed reassurance about the value of their year's work in terms of the many dimensions expected of an English literature course. However their teacher was not in a position to offer them that support.

Media Week

The fundamental aim behind the series of afternoon workshops which came to be known as 'Media Week' — led by theatre director and writer Olusola Oyeleye — was to encourage the students to focus on their own perceptions as young people while being challenged to consider issues of racism in relation to themselves. I hoped their responses, and the insights they brought to their work, might indicate 'where they were at' after their year's course. While we discussed the possibility of the students being 'in role' as a Theatre-in-Education team led by Olusola — with the task of developing ideas for a television programme about racism for young people in a predominantly white area — Olusola argued strongly that being in role would promote the idea of dealing with racism only within fiction. She felt it was important for the students to know that racism mattered to her, and affected her, in her real everyday life. Furthermore, after a year in which they had been exploring issues of injustice largely within the realm of fiction, she felt they should be ready to take on board as themselves the question of

'What does racism mean to me personally?' Instead she would introduce the students to a Theatre-in-Education way of working (which would include role play) in order to develop their ideas and treatments for a programme.

In the course of the week the students were introduced to a variety of visitors, all of whom were concerned with racism in their working lives and whose particular interests linked closely with subjects tackled in *Getting to Grips with Racism*. These included a couple of teacher-trainers/authors, representatives from the British Council of Churches Race Relations Unit concerned with immigration and deportation, a community activist and finally the producer of *Getting to Grips with Racism*, Peter Evans. The students were involved in a range of activities including examining bias in children's books, interviewing the visitors in a mock television studio, developing a role play around a deportation, improvising scenes arising from a real letter by a mother detailing racist abuse in an infant school and developing their own improvisations reflecting aspects of racism affecting young people. The latter were videoed and shared with Peter Evans, who also discussed with the students his own experience of making programmes about racism.

Student responses to the week

Responses were extremely varied. Just over half the students made positive comments, with special mention of Olusola being friendly and her making the sessions lively and relaxed. Some students wrote about gaining a sense of confidence, such as Alison who added that she had learnt 'that there's not always right and wrong answers'. There were, however, reservations. Sometimes the sessions had tended, according to Alison, 'to drag on a bit'. Caroline, however, expressed a sentiment voiced by a couple of others, which requires particular attention since it on one level appears to contradict the statements of students being encouraged to be relaxed and to have confidence in expressing themselves:

> 'No body really dared to have a go at or 'chalange' Sola or the guests. I think we were afraid that she was going to cut us off and have a go at us for thinking the way we feel.'

This was obviously a major impression for Caroline to which she returned in her evaluation paper:

> 'It was interesting but I felt that knowbody wanted to say anything that was wrong or would hurt anybodys feelings... I think Sola was a bit overpowering. If we said one thing out of line of something she didn't really agree with she would jump down our throats. She was very friendly though.'

Dan also confirmed that 'Some people didn't say their true feelings about a certain topic because they thought it might hurt Sola.'

Caroline's perceptions are particularly important to consider for two reasons. The first is that Caroline generally responded in an open and sensitive way. The second is that I could find no evidence of Olusola 'cutting off' anyone or being directly and personally critical. For instance in the first session, when she asked for responses to *Getting To Grips With Racism*, she attempted to incorporate the negative responses to the programme in a positive way:

SOLA: What did you feel about the programmes?

JOHN: I thought they were a bit one-sided.

SOLA: Right, in what way?

JOHN: Well they were always against the whites. I'm not being racist (background murmurs and giggles) but they seemed to only look at the bad points of what the white people were doing.

SOLA: In the programme what would you like to have seen then?

JOHN: Well sort of the whole story, you know, everyone's side of the story.

SOLA: Right.. so from your own point of view if you were going to create a programme like that, what might you try to do in your treatment of it?

JOHN: Well I'd show the things that can help the blacks coming to England and stuff like that.

SOLA: Right so that's an aspect that you could do and work on too. Any other ideas? Come on, go for it!

While maintaining this collaborative manner throughout the week, Olusola nevertheless made it very clear, however, that racism concerned her and she was direct in asking students to clarify their own thoughts and feelings in relation to it. That was the challenge. Her directness is evident in the following extract:

SOLA: Can I just ask a question? Do any of you believe there is any racism in the school you are attending now?

GRAHAM: No. There's no coloured people in our school.

VOICES: Yes there are.

GREG: Yes.. sometimes in jokes.

SOLA: You think so?

GREG: In jokes.

SOLA: In jokes. OK. What else? I mean... do you believe that there are any people who have racist attitudes in this school? You said um because there aren't any black people.. yeah?

GRAHAM: Not many black people.. so.. I don't think that.. you know.. I don't think they have any racist attitudes.

SOLA: So do you have to have black people for there to be racism?

GRAHAM: Yeah.

VOICES: No.

By the end of the discussion students had identified a number of areas in which racism was evident within their own environment. While clearly setting the agenda, Olusola appeared to be encouraging them to acknowledge and clarify their responses rather than to be imposing her own. With no apparent evidence of Olusola actually 'cutting off' students, and bearing in mind that Caroline also perceived Olusola as 'friendly', from where did Caroline develop her impression of Olusola 'jumping down their throats'?

Perceptions of 'one-sidedness' and anti-white bias

Evaluation revealed that a common perception existed amongst all the students that the week was, as John put it, 'one-sided'. It would appear that the messages which Olusola and the visitors conveyed were perceived primarily as coming from a perspective seen to 'favour' black people, rather than as a perspective which sought to reflect fundamental values such as justice and equality. Had the focus of the week been on the dangers of child abuse, for instance, it seems unlikely that the notion of 'one-sidedness' would have even arisen. Thus the concept of 'balance' tends to be selectively applied according to the viewers' frames of reference.

Only three students, however, wrote completely negative evaluations of the week — Ian, John and Justin. While John maintained that only a few white people discriminate (implying that the week was making an unnecessary fuss), Ian wrote that 'all that came across was that blacks are good and whites are bad. Is this true? Answer no not always.' Justin perceived almost all of the visitors to have 'absolutely totally no doughts [doubts]' and to have been 'racist against whites'.

Perceptions of an anti-white bias were, however, also expressed by students who were generally open:

'Sola gave me the impression that she thought the whole white population were against blacks! (especially us).' (Tanya)

'Sola only covered the way we treat blacks, the bad way not the good.' (Erica)

Neil, a generally thoughtful student, wrote:

'It seemed as though Sola was saying that it was just whites that could be racists... and the black could not be racist back because in their native language there weren't the words to call whites. I think that it was a poor excuse because the people in the forefront of racism are living in England or English speaking country, where there are words to call us.'

Neil's comments refer to an intense debate about language which arose amongst the adults on the final day after the teacher intervened to contest a statement by Peter Evans that it was appalling how English vocabulary was full of words of abuse for black people. Alan Parsons' view that this simply showed 'the richness of the language', was in turn contested by Olusola:

A.P.: Well the history of the country itself and its culture are of course inextricably interwoven. I mean----

SOLA: Right, so therefore the history of the country... is based on slavery.. and is based on racism. I mean look at the history of the country and look at the development of the language... You are talking about the fact that it's the richness of the language. We're talking about what those words mean, yeah? So what's that transmitted to the young people who are being taught?...

A.P.: Well obviously richness in the sense of variety.. that's exactly what I said. I said... one of the characteristics of the English language as a language is that it's a language that is full of synonyms. I mean inevitably... one of the bad consequences is bound to be that you can have synonyms for abuse as well as everything else.

In the context in which the debate arose, Alan Parsons was probably perceived by his students as rallying to the cause of 'English' and 'the English', seen to be under attack. It is unlikely that they realised they were actually also in the midst of a significant debate concerning 'knowledge about language' — a component of the English National Curriculum — and the extent to which language can be properly understood when abstracted from its social context. In the circumstances, it was not surprising that Neil interpreted Olusola's comparison between terminology in Nigeria and England to mean she believed that 'it was just whites that could be racist'. He did not take on board the point, reinforced in particular by Peter Evans, of the considerable discrepancy in the number of abusive words associated with being black and with being white within the English language itself.

Returning to my original question about the source of Caroline's perception that Olusola was ready to 'jump down our throats' and the general sense of 'one-sidedness', we need to ask whether these perceptions could have been allayed or addressed in some way, since they functioned as barriers to students opening themselves out to new learning. On the one hand Olusola wanted the students to consider what racism meant to them personally. On the other hand, without the ability to distance themselves through a wider historical and social understanding, students cannot possibly examine in a rational way how racism affects the experiences and perceptions of everyone who lives in a racist society. While there is the need for personal commitment and involvement in addressing racism, understanding can only derive from a conception of racism broadened beyond the realm of individual attitudes, morality and guilt.

There was also a feeling amongst some students that for some students the topic was now seen simply to be a 'message' which they already 'knew'. While this may have been a defensive psychological mechanism to justify a lack of interest, this response may also have been partly due to the week becoming too 'top heavy' for some students who felt themselves overloaded with 'input'. The problem was partly one of assuming the students to be more advanced in their awareness than was actually the case. In retrospect it was possible to see that, as with the television programmes, it would have been preferable to have reduced the number of visitors in order to allow the students more time to get an active grasp of one or two issues, rather than expecting them to be ready to make connections across the wider range.

Furthermore, questions raised by students about the universal nature of racism and targets of oppression other than black people required more space for discussion, even if these reflected a defensive reaction at perceiving themselves to be the sole target for criticism. Acknowledgement that racism is a phenomenon found in many societies and is multi-layered in nature — intersecting for instance with divisions of class and gender — should deepen, rather than detract from, an examination of racism within one's own society. If questions about other forms of oppression and whether black people can be racist are openly discussed, it might also be psychologically easier for white students to begin to acknowledge the implications of living in a racist society where the major beneficiaries are white people.

The teacher's responses

The discussion that arose on the final day about language and racism indicated that it was not only students who may have felt under attack. The brief but intense debate among the adults revealed a sharp divide in perspective, the visitors looking at English in its social and historical context ('based on slavery... based on racism') and the teacher viewing it, at this point, as a largely decontextualised system ('one of the characteristics of the English language as a language is that it's a language that is full of synonyms... one of the bad consequences is bound to be that you can have synonyms for abuse as well as everything else').

While I had been increasingly aware over the year of increasing dissatisfaction on the part of the teacher in terms of what he felt to be a mismatch between the project and his customary objectives as an English teacher, in the Media Week this emerged fully into the open. In the course of being 'hotseated' about the course by the visitor Gillian Klein and the students — an idea he had himself suggested — Alan Parson revealed his fundamental scepticism about the legitimacy of the project as 'English':

> DONALD (following on from G.K.): Why hadn't we done racism before?

> ALAN PARSONS (A.P.): Because it wasn't a topic which was thought of as necessarily something that could be done in an English lesson. I mean it's this kind of topic which one presumes is taking place in other lessons like R.E. for instance. I mean it's not.. it's not really the sort of topic that English teachers think of necessarily as being related to English. Do you follow me?...

> DONALD: Mm.. So.. so why did we do it then if it's not anything to do with English?

> A.P.: Er because Mrs Trewhela came along with the idea of... doing her research and she coupled her research idea on racism with some research into what is known as reader response... that seemed to be something which was very interesting and valid from the English Department's point of view in particular.

> ......

> IAN: What did you think of doing a subject for English when you thought it should be done in R.E. when Mrs Trewhela asked you about it?

> A.P.: Bluntly I think the R.E. department could have contributed a lot more in terms of time...

Given Alan Parsons' conception of the project as not strictly 'English', it was not surprising to find some students expressing doubts, particularly in their evaluations, about what had happened to their 'English'. Referring to me in her evaluation, Tanya reflected the dilemma:

> 'I think she's helped us a lot with our self confidence. Mind you, she's mucked up our sylabis around a little. Because we are moaned at by our English teacher that we can't write proper English and we are really illiterate. But we have spent all of our time with this case.'

Once again, as observed earlier, one can see the whole literature course in danger of being reduced to a confined notion of racism, here described as 'this case'. Instead of feeling reassured that she had been introduced to a wide range of inter-connecting human experiences, which had been explored through the main English National Curriculum profile components (Speaking and Listening, Reading, Writing), Tanya had the feeling that she had lost out on 'English' — even despite her own sense of increased self-confidence.

It was fortunate however that the extent of the teacher's sense of alienation from some of the fundamental ideas behind the project only emerged fully into the open for the students at this final stage, although they had received previous intimations of his unhappiness about their standard of English. This was despite his being assured by the County English Adviser that the work being produced by the students on the course was very satisfactory. The question of the frames of reference of teachers in exploring issues of racism will be addressed in the final chapter, as well as the critical question of the overall school context affecting both teachers and students. How does one teach about equality in a structurally unequal system?

Chapter Nine

Reinforcing or challenging racism? problems and possibilities

The last chapter returned us to the essential problem facing anyone trying to teach for equality. We are attempting to change that which is already established and accepted. Before outlining a number of necessary features about teaching for equality which emerged out of the course, I would first like to consider the students' evaluations of their own learning and then the project's original aims — the extension of empathy, the challenging of racist concepts and perceptions, and the development of critical thinking about our society.

In reviewing the aims it is, however, necessary to remember that they were originally formulated on the assumption that there would be a collaborative researcher-teacher relationship. Although I could not ensure that I would find a teacher with an already well-developed awareness of racism, I did assume that someone volunteering for the project would be open to developing their own understanding alongside the students'. In other words, I envisaged a teacher who would be committed to exploring anti-racist challenges arising from the texts and be supportive to students in the process. As it was, given the actual teacher's own responses, the potential for encouraging students to engage with critical issues was not fully realised. Bearing in mind this qualification, the project as it stood nevertheless still produced some positive outcomes, in addition to highlighting a range of issues which need to be addressed by others undertaking similar work.

Student evaluations

Although the overall final picture from the students was of a course that the majority felt was of value and which contained a number of popular elements, it was not without criticism. Apart from overtly negative comments from a couple of students about the focus on racism, worries were expressed (as indicated earlier) by a number of students about their 'English' having suffered. One can only speculate on the extent to which this was a reflection of the reaction of their teacher, who began the project by openly praising the texts to be studied as worthwhile literature but ended by saying racism was a subject more appropriate to Religious Education.

The course had been extremely diverse, yet after the move from fiction into reality, an element of defensiveness and a certain closing inwards began to emerge in some students. However a central strand running through many responses was the sense of being opened up to difference — different experiences, people and perspectives — accompanied often by a sense that they might otherwise not have had this 'knowledge' of 'what actually is happening in the world' (Caroline). Peter wrote that 'it is the year I think that I have learnt most about so far in my life'. For Jacky the year had 'made me not accept everything I see or read and this is a good way of seeing things'.

A distinction obviously has to be made between the students' own evaluations of what they felt they had learnt and their actual learning, as well as real changes in their perceptual frames of reference and behaviour. While long-term assessment was outside my scope, the survey was an attempt to review racist perceptions. As mentioned in Chapter Two, given the increase in average scores across the year group, the project appeared to have acted as some kind of buffer to a similar increase in explicit racism for the majority of the project students, with the girls' average score actually decreasing. The exceptions were a couple of male students whose racist views became more entrenched and the student Carl, whose sharp shift towards explicit racism from the non-racist end of the scale suggested possibly an anti-authority reaction. It is important to recognise not only contradictions within an individual's thinking but that adolescent responses are capable of fluctuation. Nevertheless, given that Carl's responses at times indicated empathy with characters in the novels who experienced racism, the notion that we can address racism simply by extending empathy through literature is clearly problematic.

The extension of empathy

Evidence of empathy within the project was based on my subjective assessment of students' involvement with the text from what they said or wrote. This evidence also needs to be viewed in the context of the construction of responses — albeit for the most part unconsciously — according to what was perceived by different students as 'appropriate' both in terms of literary, social and moral norms (Eagleton 1985).

At least three notable examples of gender differences across the class emerge from the reader-response material. First, when reading *Friedrich*, 39 per cent of the boys compared with 17 per cent of the girls suggested they would advise the narrator to hand over the rabbi to the authorities, on the basis of self-preservation. The second example occurred when the students were asked to determine whether the narrator's parents were guilty of not trying to offer more protection to Friedrich's family against the Nazis. At least 89 per cent of the boys found them not guilty on the grounds that they had acted in terms of self-preservation. In contrast, only 34 per cent of the girls decided they were not guilty or only partially guilty. However the majority of girls, who felt the narrator's family should have done more to protect their Jewish neighbours, showed more uncertainty and self-conflict in coming to their decision than most of the boys who at least in appearance were clear-cut in their pragmatism and operation of self-interest. It also seems noteworthy that the only boys in the class who were not prepared to exonerate the narrator's family turned out to have Jewish relatives themselves.

Since many of the students who exonerated the narrator's family had nevertheless displayed earlier signs of not only empathy, but sympathy, with Friedrich and his family, how did they reconcile the two positions? If the mental processes are similar to that of those who justify war while stating that any loss of life is regrettable, one needs to question the limitations of simply having 'empathy', or indeed sympathy. Writing in the context of Western responses to human destruction caused by allied forces in the Gulf War, Robert Lifton (1991) refers to the process of dissociation or 'psychic numbing, the diminished capacity or inclination to feel' through inner division of the individual mind separating out knowledge from feeling. Did most of the girls, however, tend to place a greater value on sympathetic feelings, namely that having identified and sympathised with Friedrich and his family, did they feel more obligation to give weight to the Jewish perspective? Presumably their greater uncertainty would make them susceptible to change, but were these girls at least more inclined to maintain a connection between knowledge and feeling?

The third example of a marked gender difference in responses across the class occurred in relation to *Waiting for the Rain*, when the students were asked to write personal statements to Frikkie and to Tengo after confronting each other with their conflicting perspectives. While the majority of girls clearly supported Tengo's claim for justice — thus transcending the white perspective — only a third of the boys took this position. A third of the boys remained close to the white protagonist's view and the remainder were undecided.

Here again would be an interesting area for further investigation. To what extent were boys rooted in the white perspective because of Frikkie as a young white male? If the protagonists were female, would responses have been different? In all three examples of gender differences quoted above, to what extent are the majority of female responses possibly reflective of these girls having been socialised to a greater degree than the boys into empathising with others in positions different from their own? Are their responses reflective of a greater desire to apply, or be seen to apply, over-arching principles of morality?[1] If this is so, then we need to enquire how this process functions and develops in young readers.

Thus while it is possible to state that the books read on the project all revealed the potential to engage and extend empathy amongst white students, both male and female, the study nevertheless threw up a number of questions relating empathy to issues of gender. However, in relation to exploring issues of racism, one of the clearest examples of the limitations in considering response in terms of empathy alone is provided by a student such as Michael. While showing what appeared to be genuine concern within the fiction to characters experiencing overt racism, he maintained a medium high score on the Racist Perceptions Survey and a conception of racism strictly limited to notions of personal hostility. One is reminded of Hall's statement about the deep resistance of racism 'to attempts at amelioration, good feeling, gentle reform' (Hall 1981: 61).

Challenges to racist assumptions and concepts

While the educative potential of literature is considerable, it relies on the meeting of minds — Louise Rosenblatt's 'transaction' (1978). Literature written from a strongly anti-racist perspective is in itself unlikely to be sufficient to challenge racist assumptions except for those in some way already open and ready to hear. Even where a reader's empathies are extended across previous boundaries — where sympathy has perhaps even been aroused for a character or characters usually viewed as 'other' by the reader — this does not mean a reader will automatically shift the boundaries of 'otherness'. It is more likely that Gordon Allport's 're-fencing device' (1954: 23) will operate, by which an 'exception' is acknowledged so that any break in a predetermined mental field is hastily mended. Given that the 'some of my best friends are Jews' syndrome happens frequently in real life, re-fencing is likely to be achieved with even more facility in relation to characters or situations encountered in fiction.[2]

Nevertheless over the year there were instances when racist assumptions and concepts appeared to have been successfully challenged. What would be difficult to untangle would be the direct effect of the literature itself as distinct from activities linked to it or indeed extraneous factors. For instance, once the students had interacted with Millie Murray, whose specific brief was to challenge racist assumptions in the students' construction of characters and situations in *Buddy* and *Roll of Thunder, Hear My Cry*, that experience would have been integral to any further responses. Even the activity of being asked to write a specific response, which inevitably requires an element of focusing and reflection, constitutes an intervention in the text.

As with the first aim concerning the extension of empathy, the literature chosen appeared to have considerable potential for challenging aspects of racist thinking and generating a sense of 'new learning' for a number of students. Examples have been quoted in earlier chapters, indicating a move beyond empathy into some kind of reperception and shift in frame of reference, some containing an emotive and personal force which I think significant. There was Louise who felt 'angry and embaressed to admit to myself that my South African cousins are like that...' after reading *Waiting for the Rain* and Paul who wrote how *Roll of Thunder, Hear My Cry* was 'powerful and sad, quite clearly one of the most brilliant books I've ever read'. It had given him 'a new perspective' on the treatment of black people.

Yet as with empathy, there are obviously qualifications and questions concerning the extent and effect of experiences of reperception. To what extent, for example, do individual instances of reperception begin to 'add up'? Furthermore, when they do begin to connect — as seems to be the case with Paul's sense of 'a new perspective' — will this actually inform any aspects of everyday life for him? Or is he just becoming a product of Eagleton's 'moral technology of Literature', namely 'an historically peculiar form of human subject who is sensitive, receptive, imaginative and so on... about nothing in particular' (Eagleton 1985: 5).

I should like to argue that the responses of Louise and Paul are 'particular' and at least provide a basis for further action. Reading *Waiting for the Rain* certainly caused Louise to reflect on her own South African cousins, their attitudes and behaviour in a meaningful way. Indeed the very act of attempting to make explicit such responses and changes perceived in themselves was, I believe, a step forward for these students. Admittedly we only have, as it were, their 'internal evidence' of change, but without external evidence to the contrary, it still deserves credit. Before returning to issues of the relevance of new learning in reviewing the project's third aim however, I first wish to look at the matter of negative responses and students becoming further entrenched in their racist frameworks.

It has sometimes been queried whether teaching about 'race' is advisable if it is likely to have a positive effect only on those who are already more open-minded, and likely to deepen the negative reactions of those with already closed minds. In other words, is it worth achieving what often appear to be only small shifts in a positive direction in some students if the price is to create at the same time others who become 'better-informed racists'? Although our understanding has increased of the pedagogy, context and fundamental conditions necessary for anti-racist teaching to avert the harmful effects revealed by Miller (1967; 1969) of a short dose of liberal studies teaching about 'race' to male day-release apprentices, nevertheless the problem can be a real one. This is especially so if the conditions under which a teacher is working are substantially constrained. However, given at least a reasonable amount of control over teaching circumstances, the choice as it is presented above is over-simplistic.

Firstly, one can argue that many results in education are frequently not immediately observable. It is quite possible that the effect of a learning experience may not be apparent until some time later. Secondly, while there are undoubtedly students for whom prejudice is, as Allport wrote, 'lock-stitched into the very fabric of personality' (Allport 1954: 408) in what I would regard as a pathological sense, through providing a buttress for low self-esteem and a sense of inadequacy, for many it does not serve such a specific psychological function. Put another way, the majority of white children brought up in a racist society are not personally vicious or psychologically inadequate. While racism is undoubtedly 'lockstitched' into the very fabric of our society and its culture and thus the frames of reference through which children are encouraged to view their world — so helping to shape a predominant national identity — the fabric fortunately contains other strands and its culture contains other voices, offering alternative constructions of reality.

Certainly students who tend towards openness need exposure to other voices and other ways of seeing, just as much as those who tend towards being closed and intolerant. It is precisely those students for whom there is most chance of understanding that 'race' is a lens through which they have been socialised to view themselves and others — as well as a chance of realising that they are in a position to reshape their own lenses. Because students who are intolerant tend to dominate classroom space, our work in classrooms, and indeed our own judgements of the success or failure of that work, can become unduly dominated by their responses. We need to guard against this and try to create classrooms where reflection and flexibility of mind are given status. Changing one's mind after listening to a reasoned argument should be particularly valued. While there was evidence in the project of students on occasions revising racist assumptions and concepts there was little joint reflection on this and only a small amount of time was spent in the crucial area of deconstruction of images, which I shall discuss shortly.

Development of critical thinking about society
The third aim — relating to the development of critical thinking about the nature of our society — is probably the most difficult to achieve. Dependent on realisation of the first two aims — extension of empathy and the challenging of racist notions — in the project it was concerned with the degree to which the students could be led by means of the selected literature into looking critically at their own society and thus at themselves in their own community. Circumstances led to the British context being addressed rather more directly than originally planned and it was in this final section

of the course, in which the students were being asked to move from fiction to reality, that some defensive responses began to emerge, and indeed in the case of a few students to crystallise.

The major question remains of how to create a supportive framework for challenging racism and the racist society to which the young people belong in ways that enable them to question, and indeed change, aspects of their own identity. The problem is that while racism is seen as something 'out there', it can perhaps be faced and decried. But it is another matter when it is identified as something functioning 'in here' i.e. in one's own school or worse still, in one's own head. This was the particular challenge presented to the students by Olusola Oyeleye in the final Media Week and it clearly caused some disturbance.

Related to this difficulty of looking at themselves and the part they themselves play in relation to society, was the significant lack of socio-historical awareness, not just in the project class but across the whole year group. In the second survey, with students fourteen to fifteen years old and some in their penultimate year of school, only one out of 177 referred directly to the experience of colonial domination in response to the statement 'When I think of Irish/Asian/West Indian people...' This ignorance and ignoring would appear to be intimately linked with Stuart Hall's depiction of the marginalisation of racist issues in Britain and the 'attempt to wipe out and efface every trace of the colonial and imperial past' (Hall 1978: 25). Within this overall national context, it is undoubtedly difficult to enable white students to understand racism in a social and historical context to which they themselves are inextricably connected, even if they do not personally harbour feelings of hostility.

Moving Forward

Despite limitations and constraints within the project itself, there were however not only ways in which it was evident that some students had moved forward in their thinking but it was also possible to identify a number of features — or lessons to be learnt — relating to the course, pedagogy, teacher and school which could help to effect change. There is a need for:

- a culturally diverse curriculum
- a combined focus on language and literature
- students to deconstruct their own 'knowledge'
- the integration of cognitive and affective learning
- learning to connect with the students' own experiences
- the creation of space for girls' voices
- development of a pedagogy which encourages self-esteem, open-mindedness and collaboration
- teachers to be both supportive and challenging
- teachers to develop their own awareness of racism

— the wider school context to reflect the collaborative, supportive but challenging context of the classroom.

The need for a culturally diverse curriculum

While the books read on the course were not a typical selection for a year's reading at St Mary's at the time (all of them being new additions to department stock), they would not have been an unusual combination in many London schools for instance. Given the generally high level of engagement of the project students with the texts and the positive journal comments written by most students in their final reviews of the various books, English teachers in predominantly white areas need to question the basis on which they are selecting literature. To what extent has their own reading been limited to the traditional English canon and how much have they extended their own knowledge of the rich variety of literature in English? By restricting the canon, we not only restrict our access to other voices but indeed our conceptions of humanity.

Suzanne Scafe writes of 'the value to all students of an English curriculum which is culturally diverse and receptive to change and innovation' (Scafe 1989: 3). While she is referring to the integral value of diversity for a culturally inclusive English curriculum which is capable of change and redefinition, the term 'multicultural literature' frequently indicates an approach whereby books featuring black or ethnic minority characters are merely tacked on to the static mainstream of traditional literature. A crucial feature of the project was that the students were introduced to the books not as 'multicultural', but as part of a normal English course. In other words they were introduced as works of literature in their own right, fully meeting departmental criteria for Year 9 texts. If 'multicultural literature' is to have any valid meaning, we need to reconceptualise it to embrace the whole of an English department's stock — including the diversity of Shakespeare, Jane Austen and D.H. Lawrence along with, for instance, Chinua Achebe, Alice Walker and R.K.Narayan.

The need for a combined focus on language and literature

While it was agreed from the beginning that half the students' English time would be devoted to the literature course and that the rest of their English work would remain separate to accommodate other aspects of the curriculum, the separation of work on literature and on language is an artificial one. Literature is a construction of experience — by the writer for the reader. What has been read has been written, with language both the writer's tool and scaffolding. As Pam Gilbert reminds us, 'Far from being a transparent medium, language is ideologically constructed' (Gilbert 1987: 248). With literature providing a powerful means of entry into the imagined experience of others, at the vitally important affective as well as cognitive level, a focus on the language of literature should aim to help students investigate some of the ways in which that experience has been ideologically and culturally shaped. Furthermore, what are the ways in which their own perceptions and responses are shaped by the language they themselves receive and use?

While arguing for the need for a combined focus on literature and language in English work, I am thus also arguing for students to become more conscious of themselves as language users and learners, constantly extending their own abilities with words. When students spend time talking to each other about their responses, they should not be left to feel (as did some of the project students) that this activity might be detracting from their progress in writing.

The need for students to deconstruct their own 'knowledge'

An extremely useful, although brief, specific focus on language was carried out in relation to *Waiting for the Rain,* when students were asked to compare two versions of South African history (Chapter Six, p.92). This examination of the construction of value-laden images could be extended to visual texts and developed into a wider active investigation into the language used in their own sources of history e.g. books, newspapers, television programmes. In this kind of study students would be encouraged to ask questions about selection, the power to select and the effect these selections have on their own constructions of 'knowledge'. Similar work could be linked equally well to *Friedrich* or *Roll of Thunder, Hear My Cry.* As authors writing specifically for young people, Richter and Taylor both offer voices of resistance against the imposition of authorised history and the theme emerges within each novel.

Enabling students to begin to deconstruct their own knowledge, and particularly their own racist knowledge, is to introduce them not only to a fundamental cognitive skill, but to a means of dealing constructively with that sense of moral guilt which frequently produces defensiveness. Understanding how their perceptions, and those of their parents and grandparents before them, reflect frames of reference within the society — and how these are shaped by historical events — provides students with a distancing mechanism from guilt about the past, but at the same time does not free them from responsibility for the present. A pedagogical framework with this aim in mind needs to place students actively at the centre of their own learning. Otherwise they are simply being offered one authorised version for another, a theme I shall pursue further in relation to questions of pedagogy.

The need to integrate cognitive and affective learning

Enabling students to create links between the study of history and of literature considerably enriches the potential for learning. Carl's comment that *Friedrich* had brought home to him that 'the Jews who died during the time of the Nazi dictatorship were real people and not only facts and figures' was particularly telling, as was his final question 'what the subject of the persecution of the Jews has to do with us and why in History matters like this are only skipped over without touching the heart of the matter.' What he is referring to here is the essential alienation of cognitive from affective knowledge, not simply as a process of 'psychic numbing' in response to particular events (Lifton 1991) but as a process of dissociation which is deeply structured within our society, just one indication of which is its traditional Science/Arts divide. While Carl was suggesting that the novel *Friedrich* took him into the 'heart', it would appear that for him History only entered the 'head'. Yet unless we can draw on students' hearts and give those feelings of human connection combined status with the head, the question 'what has this to do with us' is not surprising.

The students' puzzlement at taking part in a science lesson linked to the course emphasises the point about our transmission of selected constructions of 'knowledge' through traditionally defined 'subjects' embedded within the school structure. Yet racism is intricately woven into life and any serious attempt to follow the threads will take one across compartmental boundaries. Since the National Curriculum enshrines subject boundaries in law, we clearly need to hold on firmly to its notion of 'preparation for life in a multicultural society' as a 'cross-curricular dimension' which should permeate all aspects of the curriculum (NCC 1990). We need to develop sharing across subject boundaries and to encourage cross-class conversations both of staff and students. Cross-curricular work on National Curriculum themes and dimensions can provide a useful starting point.

The need to connect with the students' own experience

The popularity of the novels suggests the students found points of connection with the 'interior fiction' (Meek 1980) of the young protagonists. Furthermore the general popularity of drama seemed to derive from the greater freedom it provided for students to determine their activity and thus build on with their own experience. It is, of course, extremely difficult to assess the 'internal action' of participants within drama, let alone assess any longer term 'external' results. However the fact that learning is not immediately visible or measurable does not mean that it is not taking place, nor does it diminish the potential for drama to unite affective and cognitive learning and to draw on the students' own experience as a way of getting under the skin of someone else.

The need to create space for girls' voices

Many of the project findings have gender implications. We need not only to create spaces in which girls feel confident in expressing themselves in mixed classrooms, such as occurred in small group discussions and through reading journals, but we need to find ways in which those voices can be heard out loud and become a greater influence in creating the culture of the classroom.

A notable feature of the project class was the sharp contrast in the degree of female participation in whole class discussions as opposed to small group discussions. In the former, conducted in teacher-centred question-and-answer style, only a minority of girls ever volunteered an answer or opinion. This contrasted also with their use of the reading journals, in which they generally wrote more prolifically than most of the boys. Interviews with the girls suggested they were generally far more conscious of being 'shown up' in public than many of the boys and were thus less willing to enter into adversarial style debate, even when they knew there was not necessarily a right or wrong answer.

Fortunately both small group discussions and responding in reading journals offered the students space to express themselves in varying degrees of privacy. The reading journals served a particularly useful function as a space for self-reflection and for articulating sensitive responses they might not wish to make public. As Louise wrote: 'It's easier to write down what you think and how you feel.' Important as it is to have a range of alternative spaces for expression, these are still not a full solution to male dominance within the classroom.

Given that the project girls tended to score towards the non-racist end on the scale of Racist Perceptions and that various researchers are suggesting a greater tendency amongst girls to be more open-minded and tolerant (Chapter Two, p.31), it is of prime importance to ensure that their voices are heard in the wider classroom. Issues of gender appear closely linked with those of 'race'. We need to know more about how different socialisation processes, as well as the experience of sexism, affects the openness of white students to addressing issues of racism. Reporting on a project aimed at reducing prejudice amongst London primary school children, Phil Cohen (1987: 11) writes that:

> Gender was... a highly significant variable in the pattern of response in both schools. Boys consistently displayed more overt and extreme forms of racism or ethnocentrism than girls. Girls were much more likely to identify with other oppressed groups, and to construct story lines in which 'every underdog has its day'. They also showed much greater confidence in handling the photostory and drama work, and used these symbolic forms to explore dynamics of conflict in personal relations; the boys in contrast, were much more likely to act out rather than represent such conflicts...

Cohen's commentary carries many resonances for my own research, despite the dissimilarity in the project areas, suggesting deeply embedded differences in male and female response patterns and modes of learning. The implications are wide-ranging, reinforcing the notion that it is impossible to tackle racism effectively in isolation. Put bluntly, if a predominantly white classroom and school give priority to white male experience, what is the likelihood that racism can be properly addressed? If Chris Gaine (1987: 46) is correct in his assertion that girls are easier to teach about 'race' than boys, what are the implications? While I did not set out with a particular focus on gender and my project does not provide the systematic testing which Gaine acknowledges is necessary, nevertheless it tends to bear him out. This is surely a key area for further work and has important implications for pedagogy.

Questions of pedagogy

While the project methodology ensured a certain amount of space both for student autonomy and collaborative learning, the personal style of the teacher who undertook the project turned out to be predominantly didactic, traditionally formal, and by his own acknowledgement disciplinarian. As already mentioned, whole class discussions were largely male-dominated. My observations strongly reinforce the findings of others in the field about the importance of establishing an appropriate classroom context for raising issues of racism. In addressing racism with white students, one is challenging them not only to extend their range of empathy but to question their frames of reference and thus elements of their own identities. It is therefore essential to create an ethos in which trust and respect form the basis for developing the self-esteem necessary to undertake such self-critical activity. In order to promote open-mindedness in students, it has also to be practised, and one therefore requires an ethos of tolerance. Finally, there is little point talking about equality and the inter-dependence of human beings if students are not encouraged to collaborate with each other.

The role of the teacher

Within the kind of pedagogical framework I am outlining as necessary for addressing racism, the role of the teacher is undoubtedly a difficult one. It is one both of support and challenge. Unless the teacher can create a trusting and supportive atmosphere, students will merely become defensive. And unless there is challenge, students will remain unchanged. Furthermore if the students are to come to understand that racism is not just a matter of negative and nasty attitudes and feelings, but that 'race' is a pervasive social lens which is constantly shaping much of their 'knowledge', then they need to see their teacher involved in the same process of questioning and self-scrutiny. The teacher has to enable what is often hidden and submerged, to come to the surface. The teacher who expects students to combine affective with cognitive knowledge, needs likewise to be prepared to offer heart as well as head.

In short, the teacher is an essential element within her or his own pedagogical framework. To help create trust leading to self-esteem, tolerance leading to open-mindedness and collaboration leading to a respect for equality, the teacher has to practise all those qualities.

Of the pedagogical skills outlined here, most are not specific to anti-racist teaching but a reflection of a broadly liberal approach to education. However, in relation to anti-racist teaching there is also the central question of the teacher's own level of awareness about racism. A teacher who perceives racism only at the obvious personal or behaviourial level will not be able to take students very far. A teacher who has not begun to examine how living in a society culturally seeped in racism for centuries has infiltrated their own substratum of beliefs, assumptions, perceptions and values, will not be in a position to help students engage in that difficult and often uncomfortable task. A teacher who has not begun to examine how racism is Hall's 'structured absence' (Hall 1985), as well as how it is deeply embedded within the structures and institutions of our society, will not be in a position to help students uncover these realities.

Apart from the question of awareness in relation to the content of anti-racist teaching, there are also a range of issues which teachers need to consider carefully, for example responses to racist language and behaviour. Although the pedagogical framework may be one based on trust, tolerance and collaboration, there needs to be recognition of the wider framework of the entitlement of all to equal treatment and that racist abuse constitutes illegal discrimination. Teachers, and indeed schools, need to be very clear about policies and procedures for response and these need to be made explicit to students.

While teachers needs to be extremely clear on the latter, regardless of whether they are teaching about racism, it is difficult to specify just what level of awareness a teacher should have reached before beginning to engage students directly in the issues. However desirable it is that teachers should have undergone their own process of awareness-raising in advance, it is unrealistic to think this represents the reality of teaching. One cannot assume that the majority of white English teachers reading *Roll of Thunder, Hear My Cry* with their students will necessarily have read much else by black writers, nor thought in any depth about a black perspective or, as the project teacher acknowledged prior to the project, about racism. How many teachers would, like the project teacher and students, similarly feel the Logans were being somewhat unfair to Jeremy by not equally reciprocating his efforts at friendship? How many might feel that Joseph in *Waiting for the Rain* was not being fair to the white liberal family who helped pay for his education? In other words, how many would be using the criterion of 'balance' without understanding the fundamental imbalance of power between white and black in each situation?

In being faced with such questions, for some people there may only be a fine line between acknowledging one's lack of understanding and a demoralising sense of inadequacy, which can lead to white teachers feeling they are not capable of teaching works by black writers. It is not my intention to suggest the latter, but to point to the need for white teachers to engage in the process of extending their own reading and insights at an adult level and to acknowledge themselves as co-learners in the process of reperception. Sharing the interest and stimulation of opening themselves out to the voices of black writers and new perspectives is probably the most valuable quality they could pass on to their students.

The school context

The collaborative, supportive context which I have outlined as prerequisite for challenging racism in the classroom clearly needs to be reflected in the school as a whole. Addressing inequality needs to be an ongoing, long-term commitment which is integral to the curriculum both formal and informal. A written school philosophy rejecting racism, however sincerely held by a Headteacher and some individual members of staff, cannot be effective without a structured mechanism whereby the implications of this statement are addressed throughout the school. While individual initiatives (such as the project) are vital and require space, there needs to be a challenge and an impetus towards change in the wider school, accompanied by the creation of collaborative structures for discussing, reflecting on and expanding those initiatives.

Rigid subject disciplines and hierarchies militate against developing an ethos which values equality, as does a system of banding. Although a school may not be single-mindedly concerned with academic performance, rather aiming to recognise a broad range of qualities and abilities amongst its students, the maintenance of a banding structure inevitably affects students' perceptions of themselves and others at a fundamental level by reinforcing concepts of ranking. The connection between collaborative learning frameworks and prejudice reduction has far-reaching implications throughout a school (King 1986). Furthermore, if students are to value equality and justice, do they themselves not need to be involved in helping develop such a policy, as well as monitoring and sustaining it?

The difficulties of addressing racism in a predominantly white school were well illustrated in St Mary's. Senior management were reluctant to commit in-service time to a multicultural/anti-racist agenda unless it was in response to staff requests. Quite genuinely they feared that without initial staff interest, any in-service work would provoke resistance and prove counter-productive. With continually increasing pressure on teachers within schools at a time of unprecedented educational change, senior staff stated that it was crucial to give priority to teachers' perceived curriculum needs. Since the common conception of racism was to do with personal hostility, and since there was little overt evidence of this in St Mary's, with its few black students appearing to all intents 'well integrated' into a generally harmonious environment, it seemed unlikely that teachers would indeed perceive a need for an anti-racist focus. The notion that prejudice and racism would normally be dealt with in Religious Education, as overtly expressed in the final week by the project teacher, appeared widely held.

Given the lack of any open forum where these issues were aired, I can only surmise that few teachers recognised that if ideas of social justice are to become real in the lives of the students, they need to be woven not only into the whole curriculum but into all aspects of school life. However, a significant factor in the teachers' perceptions has to be their own sense of themselves in relation to issues of equality and justice. With the establishment of increasingly centralised political control over education by the Conservative right, teachers were subjected in the 1980s to a steady process of social devaluation, culminating in the loss of their negotiating rights with the 1987 Pay and Conditions Act and the 1988 Education Reform Act (Jones 1989).

Ideas of equality and justice cannot be adequately addressed in classrooms alone. They need to pervade the corridors leading to all corners of the school including the staffroom, senior management offices, canteen and kitchens. Indeed they need to extend outside the school gates, through school governors, parents and students into the 70,000 hours of a child's life beyond the 15,000 hours spent in school (Heath and Clifford 1980).

Final thoughts

While English teachers are fortunate not to have a content-prescriptive National Curriculum and to have features in the English document which can be used to positive advantage, one should nevertheless recall Ken Jones' critique about the recommendation of progressive methodology cut off from its original 'radical, social and cultural commitments' (Jones 1990). It is essential we retain the sense of education as a means of 'opening out' and liberation and resist the essential segmentation of 'knowledge' into separate subjects, profile components and attainment targets. Writing of the need to address the structural inequalities of race, class and gender, Hazel Taylor (1984) uses the metaphor of an old-fashioned cupboard in her head with three doors. We have to learn how to keep open the three doors simultaneously so we remain aware of the inter-connections of their contents:

> 'What is an appropriate pedagogy through which to convey the values of equality for each individual? Responsibility needs to be given to pupils for their own learning, power restored to individuals, teacher mediation used to ensure equality of learning time and facilitation. Means need to be created for girls to practise as leaders, as organisers, as sources of valuable insights, for boys to practise as listeners, supporters, facilitators for discussion and social cohesion. Sexual harassment must be taken as seriously as racial harassment, sexist language be acknowledged as being as offensive as racist language. The structures of the school must support the learning in the classrooms, which means that in formulating policy it is essential collec-

tively to create democratic management arrangements, open means of consultation, a means for pupils' and the community's, as well as the teachers' voices to be heard. The structures of the school must make more explicit the meanings of equality, of sharing, of considerations for diverse views, that the classroom experience should be helping the pupils to formulate. The doors in the pupils' minds, teachers' minds, the doors of the classroom, and of the school, should stand open, always.' (Taylor 1984)

While I believe this model of open doors, with its 'the medium is the message' approach, to be the surest way forward, addressing racism in a predominantly white area presents a particular challenge. The less diversity in the community, the greater will be the sense of an implicitly white heritage which the school is expected to transmit. The school has to be very clear and explicit about the moral framework within which it is operating its policy of open doors. It cannot be a policy which legitimises the free flow of racist ideology.

This poses difficult questions in relation to a model of participatory democracy. For instance, how can one ensure that encouraging the free expression of views from the community, including inevitably racist views, does not become collusion? Church schools have a distinct advantage here over non-denominational schools in that there is already an inbuilt moral code to which parents, students and staff ostensibly subscribe. The problem in these circumstances is how to get beneath this apparent surface consensus to what people really think and feel and to create an atmosphere which will support people examining their own contradictions.

Despite all the limitations in terms of effecting change in the wider school and social context, the one-year literature-based course at St Mary's nevertheless did offer a door to further learning. Firstly, it raised a number of key questions, not only for English teachers but for all those engaged in combating racism and teaching for equality and justice. Secondly, it introduced at least some students to new areas of thought and feeling, which perhaps some of them will one day pursue.

Thirdly, but certainly not last in importance, while the project itself may only be a vague memory for the school, one small door was opened at an institutional level in that the books used on the course are now part of the regular stock in the English department. There will be other young readers who, for instance, will be affected by the power of Mildred D. Taylor's tale of black experience and make some connection with it, as did a number of the project students. As with any educational experience, what they will do with their newly aroused feelings and knowledge is uncertain, but at least they will have been opened to new voices. That, at an individual level, is a beginning.

Notes to Chapter 9

1   According to the findings of James Squire (1964), adolescent girls are slightly more inclined as readers to make prescriptive judgements than boys.

2   Michael's indecision on the second survey in response to the item 'Jokes about people from other cultures are just a bit of fun', following his close-to-tears conversation with Olusola about not meaning to be hurtful in telling such jokes, is indicative of the power of re-fencing.

Bibliography

Achebe, C. (1989) 'Travelling white', The Guardian, 22.10.89.

Acts of the Privy Council, XXVI, 1596-7. In Greater London Council (1986) A History of the Black Presence in London, London: Greater London Council.

Allport, G. (1954) The Nature of Prejudice, Reading, Massachusetts: Addison-Wesley.

Bagley, C. and Verma, G.K. (1975) 'Inter-Ethnic Attitudes and Behaviour in English Multiracial Schools', in Verma, G.K. and Bagley, C. (eds.) Race and Education Across Cultures, London: Heinemann.

Ball, W. and Troyna, B. (1989) 'The Dawn of a New ERA? The Education Reform Act, 'Race' and LEAs', Educational Management and Administration, 17: 23-31.

Bayfield, T. (1981) Churban The Murder of the Jews of Europe, London: Michael Goulston Educational Foundation.

Benton, M. (1983) 'Secondary Worlds', Journal of Research and Development in Education, 16, 3: 68-75.

Benton, M., Teasey, J., Bell, R. and Hurst, K. (1988) Young readers responding to poems, London: Routledge.

Berry, J. (1988) When I Dance, London: Hamish Hamilton.

Blishen, E. (1966) Roaring Boys, London: Panther Books.

Bolton, G. (1979) Towards a theory of drama in education, Harlow: Longman.

Bourdieu, P. (1976) 'The school as a conservative force: scholastic and cultural inequalities'. In Dale, R., Esland, G. and MacDonald, M. (eds.) Schooling and Capitalism: A Sociological Reader, Milton Keynes: Open University Press.

Bowles, S. (1976) 'Unequal education and the reproduction of the social division of labor'. In Dale, R., Esland, G. and MacDonald, M. (eds.) Schooling and Capitalism: A Sociological Reader, Milton Keynes: Open University Press.

British Broadcasting Corporation (BBC). (1988) Getting to Grips with Racism, London: BBC Television for Schools.

British Broadcasting Corporation (BBC) Scene (1988). South Africa, London: BBC Television for Schools.

British Social Attitudes, (1984) London: HMSO.

Brown, C., Barnfield, J. and Stone, M. (1990) Spanner in the Works: Education for racial equality and social justice in white schools, Stoke-on-Trent: Trentham Books.

Brutus, D. (1973) A Simple Lust: Collected Poems of South African Jail and Exile, London: Heinemann African Writers Series.

Carter, B. and Williams, J. (1987) 'Attacking racism in education'. In Troyna, B. (ed.) Racial Inequality in Education, London: Tavistock Publications.

Cohen, P. (1987) Reducing Prejudice in Classroom and Community, PSEC/CME Cultural Studies Project, London: University of London Institute of Education (mimeo).

Commission for Racial Equality (CRE). (1988) Learning in Terror: A survey of racial harassment in schools and colleges, London: Commission for Racial Equality.

Cosway, P. and Rodney, C. (1987) "Multicultural Fiction' in a Suburban School', Multicultural Teaching, 5, 2: 19-23.

Delamont, S. and Hamilton, D. (1986) 'Revisiting Classroom Research: A Continuing Cautionary Tale'. In Hammersley, M. (ed.) Controversies in Classroom Research, Milton Keynes: Open University Press.

Department of Education and Science (DES). (1989) English for ages 5 to 16 Proposals of the Secretary of State for Education and Science and the Secretary of State for Wales, National Curriculum, London: Department of Education and Science.

Dickinson, P. (1971) The Devil's Children, London: Gollancz.

Dodgson, E. (1984) Motherland — West Indian Women to Britain in the 1950s, London: Heinemann.

Eagleton, T. (1985) 'The Subject of Literature', The English Magazine, 15: 4-7.

The English Centre. (1984) Roll of Thunder, Hear My Cry (background book), London: I.L.E.A. English Centre.

The English Programme. (1984) Friedrich (video), London: Thames Television Education.

The English Programme. (1988) Roll of Thunder, Hear My Cry (video), London: Thames Television Education.

Epstein, D. and Sealey, A. (1990) 'Where it really matters..' developing anti-racist education in predominantly white primary schools, Birmingham: Birmingham Development Education Centre.

Festinger, L. (1957) A Theory of Cognitive Dissonance, Palo Alto: Stanford University Press.

Festinger, L. (1964) 'Behavioral Support for Opinion Change', Public Opinion Quarterly, 28: 404-417.

Figueroa, P.M.E. (1984) 'Race Relations and Cultural Differences: Some Ideas on a Racial Frame of Reference'. In Verma, G.K. and Bagley, C.(eds.) Race Relations and Cultural Differences, London: Croom Helm.

Figueroa, P.M.E. (1991) The Social Construction of Race, London: Routledge.

Figueroa, P.M.E. and Swart, L.T. (1986) 'Teachers' and Pupils' Racist and Ethnicist Frames of Reference: A Case Study'. In New Community, 13, 1: 40-51.

Freund, E. (1987) The Return of the reader: Reader-Response Criticism, London: Methuen.

Gaine, C. (1987) No Problem Here: A practical approach to education and 'race' in white schools, London: Hutchinson.

Gilbert, P. (1987) 'Post Reader-Response: The Deconstructive Critique'. In Corcoran, B. and Evans, E. (eds.) Readers, Texts, Teachers, Milton Keynes: Open University Press.

Gilroy, P. (1987) 'There Ain't No Black in the Union Jack', The cultural politics of race and nation, London: Hutchinson.

Gordon, S. (1987) Waiting For The Rain, London: Orchard Books.

Gramsci, A. (1971) Selections from the Prison Notebooks. Ed and trans by Hoare, Q. and Nowell Smith, G., International Publishers, New York.

Guy, R. (1977) The Friends, Harmondsworth: Puffin.

Hall, S. (1978) 'Racism and Reaction'. In Five Views of Multiracial Britain, London: Commission for Racial Equality.

Hall, S. (1981) 'Teaching Race'. In James, A. & Jeffcoate, R. (eds.) The School in the Multicultural Society, London: Harper & Row/ Open University Press.

Hall, S. (1985) Anti-racism in practice: Stuart Hall examines the implications of using ACER materials (video), Inner London Education Authority (ILEA): Afro-Caribbean Education Resource Centre (ACER).

Hammersley, M. (1983) 'Introduction: Reflexivity and Naturalism in Ethnography'. In Hammersley, M. (ed) The Ethnography of Schooling: Methodological Issues, Driffield: Nafferton Books.

Hann, S. (undated) People Connect With Each Other: The report of the FAME Fiction and Multicultural Education project, Slough: Slough Teachers' Centre.

Harding, D.W. (1962) 'Psychological Processes in the Reading of Fiction', The British Journal of Aesthetics, 2, 2: 140-4.

Hatcher, R. (1989) 'Antiracist Education after the Act', Multicultural Teaching, 7, 3: 24-7.

Hatt, F. (1976) The Reading Process: a framework for analysis and description, London: Clive Bingley.

Heath, A. and Clifford, P. (1980) 'The seventy thousand hours that Rutter left out', Oxford Review of Education, 6, 1: 3-19.

Hiernaux, J. et al. (1965) 'Biological aspects of race', International Social Science Journal, XVII, 1: 71-161.

Hinton, N. (1983) Buddy, London: Heinemann Educational.

Hollindale, P. (1988) Ideology and the Children's Book, Oxford: Westminster College/Thimble Press.

Iser, W. (1978) The act of reading: A theory of aesthetic response, London: Routledge and Kegan Paul.

Jeffcoate, R. (1979) Positive Image: Towards a multiracial curriculum, London: Writers and Readers Publishing Cooperative.

Jones, K. (1989) Right Turn: The Conservative Revolution in Education, London: Hutchinson Radius.

Jones, K. (1990) 'Equality and the National Curriculum', Multicultural Teaching, 8, 3: 16-7.

King, E. (1986) 'Recent experimental strategies for prejudice reduction in American schools and classrooms', Journal of Curriculum Studies, 18, 3: 331-8.

Klineberg, O. (1950) 'Prejudice: The Concept'. In Sills, D.L. (ed) International Encyclopaedia of the Social Sciences, The Macmillan Company & The Free Press.

Lawton, D. (1973) Social Change, Educational Theory and Curriculum Planning, London: University of London Press.

Laye, C. (1959) The African Child, London: Fontana Books.

Lee, H. (1960) To Kill a Mockingbird, Harmondsworth: Penguin.

Lester, J. The Tales of Uncle Remus: The Adventures of Brer Rabbit, London: The Bodley Head.

Lewontin, R. (1987) 'Are the Races Different?' In Gill, D. and Levidow, L. (eds.) Anti-Racist Science Teaching, London: Free Association Books.

Lifton, R.J. (1991) 'Techno-bloodshed', The Guardian, 14.2.91.

Lynch, J. (1987) Prejudice Reduction and the Schools, London: Cassell.

Marsh, A. (1976) 'Who hates the blacks?', New Society, 23.9.76: 649-52.

Meek, M. (1980) 'Prolegomena for a study of children's literature or Guess what's in my head'. In Approaches to research in children's literature, Southampton: University of Southampton, Department of Education (mimeo).

Miller, H.J. (1967) 'A study of the effectiveness of a variety of teaching techniques for reducing colour prejudice in a male student sample aged 15-21', London: University of London M.A. thesis.

Miller, H.J. (1969) 'The Effectiveness of Teaching Techniques for Reducing Colour Prejudice', Liberal Education, 16: 25-31.

Mullard, C. (1980) Racism in Society and Schools: History, Policy and Practice, Occasional Paper No 1, London: University of London Institute of Education.

Naidoo, B. (1985) Journey to Jo'burg: A South African Story, Harlow: Longman.

Naidoo, B. (1987) (ed.) Free As I Know, London: Bell and Hyman.

Naidoo, B. (1989) Chain of Fire, London: Collins.

Naidoo, B. (1991) Exploring Issues of Racism with White Students through a Literature-based Course, Ph.D. thesis, University of Southampton.

National Curriculum Council. (1990) Three: The Whole Curriculum, York: National Curriculum Council.

Needle, J. (1979) My Mate Shofiq, London: Fontana Lions.

Purves, A. and Beach, R. (1972) Literature and the Reader: Research in Response to Literature, Reading Interests, and the Teaching of Literature, Final report to The National Endowment for the Humanities. Urbana, Illinois: National Council of Teachers of English.

Ree, H. (1991) 'Improving Reading', Times Educational Supplement, 4.1.91.

Richardson, R. (undated) 'Justice and Equality in the Classroom — The Design of Lessons and Courses', World Studies Documentation Service, 7, York: World Studies Teacher Training Centre.

Richardson, R. (1988) 'Opposition to Reform and the Need for Transformation: Some Polemical Notes', Multicultural Teaching, 6, 2: 4-8.

Richardson, R. (1989) 'Manifesto for Inequality — some features of the new era', Multicultural Teaching, 8, 1: 19-20.

Richter, H.P. (1978) Friedrich, London: Heinemann Educational.

Rose, S. et al. (1978) Race, Education, Intelligence — A teacher's guide to the facts and the issues, London: N.U.T.

Rosenblatt, L. M. (1938) Literature as Exploration, New York: Appleton-Century; revised ed. (1970) London: Heinemann.

Rosenblatt, L. M. (1978) The reader, the text, the poem: The transactional theory of the literary work, Carbondale: Southern Illinois University Press.

Rosenblatt, L. M. (1985) 'The Transactional Theory of the Literary Work: Implications for Research'. In Cooper, C.R.(ed) Researching Response to Literature and the Teaching of Literature, Norwood, N.J.: Ablex.

Scafe, S. (1989) Teaching Black Literature, London: Virago.

Searle, C. (1977) Compiler of The World in a Classroom, London: Writers and Readers.

Sheppard, C. and Sauvageot, C. (1987) Girls Apart (video), Paris: New Internationalist Films/CCFD.

Squire, J. (1964) The Responses of Adolescents While Reading Four Short Stories, NCTE Research Report No.2. Champaign, Illinois: National Council of Teachers of English.

Stredder, K.N.M. (1978) 'An illuminative evaluation of a piece of multiracial curriculum implemented in a multiracial secondary school in Birmingham', Birmingham: University of Birmingham, M.Ed. thesis.

Swann Report, Department of Education and Science (1985) Education for All: the report of the Committee of Inquiry into the Education of Children from Ethnic Minority Groups, Cmnd 9453, London: HMSO.

Tatelbaum, I. (1985) Through Our Eyes: Children Witness The Holocaust (video), Jerusalem: Advanced Communications Ltd.

Taylor, B. (1984) 'Multicultural education in a monocultural region', New Community, 12, 1: 1-8.

Taylor, H. (1984) 'An Open Cupboard Policy', Issues in Race and Education, Spring 1984: 1-4.

Taylor, M.D. (1987) Roll of Thunder, Hear My Cry, London: Heinemann Educational.

Thatcher, M. (1978) 'World in Action', ITV, 30.1.1978.

Tolkien, J.R.R. 'On fairy-stories'. In Tree and leaf, London: Allen and Unwin, 1964.

Tomlinson, S. (1990) Multicultural Education in White Schools, London: Batsford.

Treacher, V. (1983) 'Teaching about race relations through literature: the use of *Black Boy* in a CSE class'. In Adelman, C. et al. A Fair Hearing for All: Relationships between teaching and racial equality, Bulmershe Publication No.2, Reading: Bulmershe College of Higher Education.

Treacher, V. (1984/5) 'Teaching Black Literature', World Studies Journal, 5, 3: 23-5.

Twitchin, J. (ed) (1988) The Black and White Media Book, Stoke-on-Trent: Trentham Books.

van Wyk, C. (1986) 'No Kidding'. In New Internationalist, May 1986.

Verma, G. K. (1990) 'Identity, Education and Black Learners: are things improving?', Multicultural Teaching, 8, 3: 18-19.

Williams, M. (1986) 'The Thatcher Generation', New Society, 21.2.86, 75: 312-15.

Wright, R. (1971) Black Boy, Harlow: Longman Imprint (first published 1945 by Victor Gollancz).

Zimet, S.G. (1980) Print and Prejudice, Sevenoaks: Hodder and Stoughton/United Kingdom Reading Association.